GIFT *of the* WHALE

The
Iñupiat
Bowhead
Hunt,
A
Sacred
Tradition

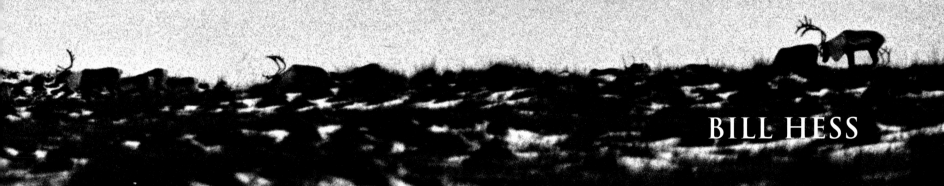

BILL HESS

Photograph on first page: A gray whale passes by Barrow. Preceding page:
Isaac Kaigelak takes aim at a caribou near the village of Nuiqsut.
Right: Rhoda Pikok with fish.

Printed in China
Published by Sasquatch Books
Distributed by Publishers Group West
08 07 06 05 04 03   5 4 3 2 1

A note about the spellings in this text: *Iñupiat* (the people) and *Iñupiaq* (the language and culture) are the preferred spellings of the Iñupiat of the Arctic Slope,
and therefore the spellings used in this text. The word *iglu* refers to the sod
homes built by the peoples of northern Alaska, as distinguished from the ice
igloos used in northeastern Canada.

Cover and book design by Karen Schober
Map illustration by Linda Feltner
Copyedited by Don Graydon

Library of Congress Cataloging in Publication Data
Hess, Bill.
        Gift of the whale : the Iñupiat bowhead hunt, a sacred
tradition / photos and text by Bill Hess.
                p. cm.
        Includes bibliographical references.
        ISBN I-57061-163-7 (hardcover) / ISBN I-57061-382-6 (paperback)
        I. Iñupiat. 2. Whaling—Alaska. 3. Bowhead whale. I. Title.
        E99.E7H4919 1999
        639.2'8'08997120798—dc2I
        99-20779

SASQUATCH BOOKS
SEATTLE
119 South Main Street, Suite 400
Seattle, WA 98104
(206) 467-4300
books@sasquatchbooks.com
www.sasquatchbooks.com

For Margie:

So quiet, almost invisible,

yet for me always there.

Without you this work would not exist.

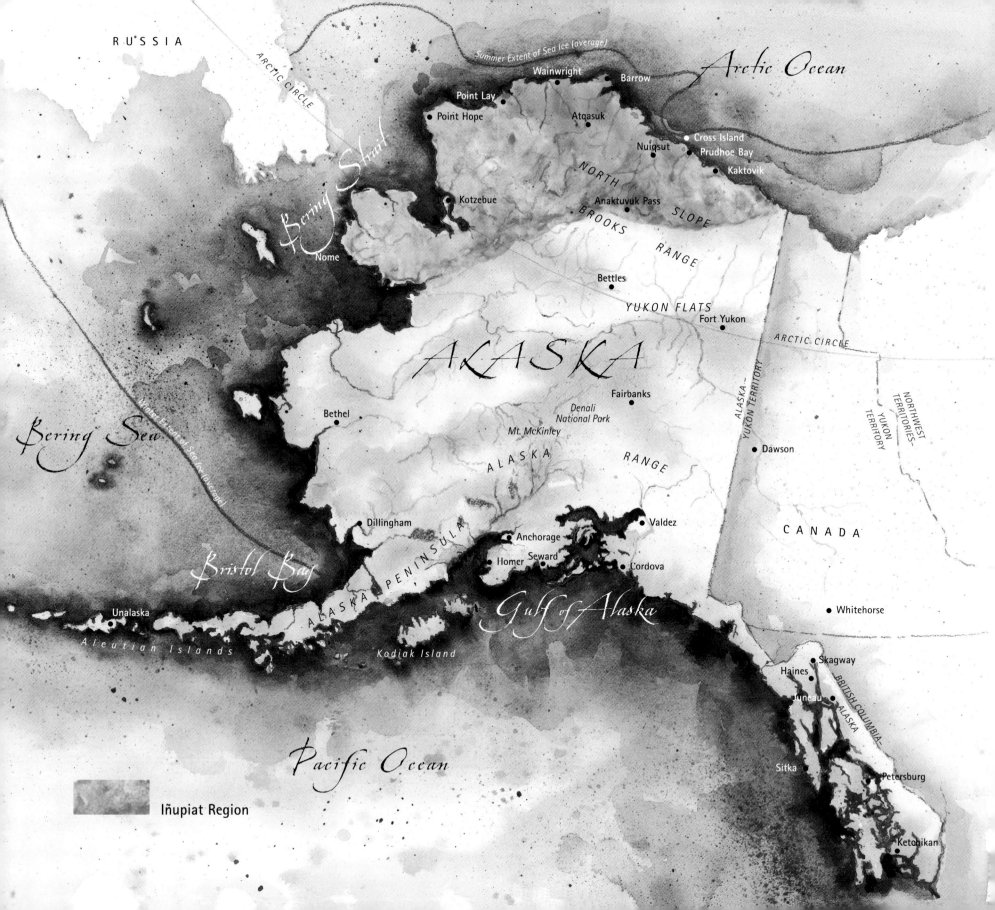

RUSSIA

ARCTIC CIRCLE

Summer Extent of Sea Ice (average)

Arctic Ocean

Wainwright

Barrow

Point Lay

Point Hope

Atqasuk

Bering Strait

Cross Island

Nuiqsut

Prudhoe Bay

Kaktovik

NORTH

SLOPE

Kotzebue

Anaktuvuk Pass

BROOKS

RANGE

Nome

Bettles

YUKON FLATS

Fort Yukon

ARCTIC CIRCLE

ALASKA

Bering Sea

Winter Extent of Sea Ice (average)

Fairbanks

Bethel

Denali National Park

Mt. McKinley

ALASKA

RANGE

ALASKA–YUKON TERRITORY

NORTHWEST TERRITORIES–YUKON TERRITORY

Dawson

CANADA

Dillingham

Valdez

ALASKA

PENINSULA

Anchorage

Homer

Seward

Cordova

Bristol Bay

Gulf of Alaska

Whitehorse

Unalaska

Aleutian Islands

Kodiak Island

Skagway

Haines

BRITISH COLUMBIA–ALASKA

Juneau

Pacific Ocean

Sitka

Petersburg

Iñupiat Region

Ketchikan

CONTENTS

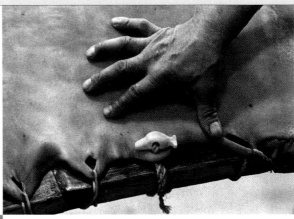

Left: Breaching bowhead whale off Point Barrow.

IT IS IMPOSSIBLE FOR ME to properly acknowledge all those who have assisted me in so many different ways during the seventeen-year course of this work. I have slept under many different roofs and in numerous tents; I have been fed countless servings of *quak, maktak, mikigaq,* and *tuttu* by more good people than I can recount; and I have been shown numerous hospitalities, both large and small. When I had no snowmachine of my own, sleds or back seats were made freely available to me; when I did have one, folks were quick to come to my aid each time I sank it in the ocean—both to help

me fish it out and then get it running again. (Sadly, after a truck ran over it, there was nothing anybody could do.) I have ridden in many boats, bummed many helicopter and airplane rides, and have given a few of the latter myself. Good women have patched my torn parka and have sewn my plane's wing covers after the wind had ripped them to shreds. Individuals fluent in both Iñupiaq and English have interpreted the words of the elders for me. Those who have shared their stories and lives with me number in the hundreds, and I have been enriched a hundred times.

I could go on and on like this and throw out scores of names—and still, I would miss scores. And I do not want to leave anyone out. Forgive me, then, beloved Iñupiat people—you of the sea, the ice, the land, the tundra grass and flowers, the animals therein and thereon, and you of the generous and giving heart—for not thanking you all by name, for you are just too numerous to do so. So, I thank you all.

To those non-Natives who have also helped me—and there have been many—I thank you as well.

"BOWHEADS ARE COMING BY about one every fifteen minutes," Simon Koonook said as he looked up from the surveyor's instrument. The son of one of the most successful whaling captains of Point Hope, Alaska, Simon had opted not to join his father's crew this year, but to lend his sharp, observant eyes to the annual whale census. From atop a thirty-foot perch of ice towering over a wide, riverlike break in the frozen ocean five miles offshore from Point Barrow, census takers had so far counted eleven hundred passing bowheads. Simon never let his intent eyes drift from the water for more than a glance. "Bowhead!" he suddenly exclaimed, pointing to the southwest.

Backlit by a hard sun, a V-shaped plume of disintegrating spray drifted over the black, rolling back of a bowhead whale. Simon dropped his eye to the instrument, sighted in on the animal, then called out distance and bearing readings, which a biologist jotted down with a pencil. "We're in the thick of the migration, right now," he said upon lifting his head again.

We were also in what should have been the thick of the bowhead whaling season. For millennia, Iñupiat hunters—skin boats and harpoons ready—had waited here at the ice edge to greet the returning bowheads, to accept their gifts of life and culture. Typically the hunt would begin in the final week of April and continue on as late as mid-June, while bowheads migrated from winter waters in the Bering Sea through the Chukchi Sea to their summer home above Canada in the Beaufort Sea. I had been told that the first week of May was especially prime; that if weather and ice conditions permitted, this would be the time the hunters of Barrow would enjoy their greatest success.

This was the first week of May 1982. Weather and ice conditions were ideal. Whales were plentiful. Yet no hunters awaited the bowheads. Under a strict quota imposed by the International Whaling Commission, Barrow had been allotted five strikes to land four bowheads. All five strikes had been made but with no whales landed. I had come as a reporter-photographer for the *Tundra Times*, an Alaska Native newspaper published out of Anchorage, hoping to cover the bowhead hunt. With no hunting going on, I had come to the bowhead census camp instead.

⸺

Iñupiat knowledgeable in their oral history say the hunt reaches back many thousands of years, deep into time immemorial. Scientists say it has been going on for more than two thousand years. With the body-warming energy and high vitamin C content of its *maktak* (the thick, black skin and the attached layer of oily blubber), the nutrition in its meat and internal organs, the bones that were used to frame sod *iglus*, the elastic baleen that was woven into fine baskets, and the liver membranes used to cover drums, the bowhead long ago took its place as the central element in the diet, culture, and spiritual well-being of the arctic coast Iñupiat. It is because of the bowhead whale that communities such as Barrow and Point Hope exist at all.

Yankee whalers first sailed into the western Arctic in 1848 to commercially hunt this fat, oily whale that can exceed sixty feet in length (a third of which is its bony head) and weigh

more than a ton per foot. Estimates place the mid–nineteenth-century bowhead population of the region at eighteen thousand to twenty thousand. Commercial whaling records indicate Yankee whalers had killed at least nineteen thousand bowheads by 1915, when depletion brought the commercial hunt to an end.

Along with its sacred bowhead, the Iñupiat population also was drastically reduced. Starvation, plus diseases brought in by the Yankee whalers, killed off half of the Iñupiat.

As both man and whale began a long recovery process, the diminished population of the Iñupiat continued hunting the reduced population of bowheads. Always resourceful, quick to adapt technology to their own needs, the Iñupiat incorporated into their traditional hunt the heavy brass, bomb-firing shoulder and darting guns introduced by the Yankee whalers. The outside world, whose need for oil, corsets, and hair ornaments had nearly wiped out the bowheads, stepped back and did little more to disturb the relationship between the Iñupiat and the bowhead.

In 1947 the International Whaling Commission was formed to regulate the commercial hunting of whales globally. The bowhead was placed on the endangered species list in 1970. Two years later, the commission asked the United States for data on the western Arctic bowhead population and on the Alaska hunt.

Congress had passed the Alaska Native

Right: Twelve-year-old Rex Rock Jr. retrieves an eider duck he shot in late May on the ice anchored off Point Hope.

Claims Settlement Act in 1971. Although Iñupiat leaders had helped instigate the land claims movement and had fought hard for a fair settlement, the act was passed in a form opposed by the Iñupiat. The settlement act dispossessed Alaska's Eskimo, Indian, and Aleut populations of 340 million acres of traditional lands, including oil-rich Prudhoe Bay, for reimbursement of just under one billion dollars. The one billion dollars in reimbursement was channeled to capitalize twelve regional and two hundred fourteen village for-profit corporations created by the act to take fee-simple title to the forty-four million acres left to the Native population.

Realizing that virtually all of the staggering wealth about to be generated from their traditional lands at Prudhoe Bay and its estimated thirteen billion barrels of recoverable oil would

■ **Left:** Where Iqilaaluk Creek flows into the Kugaagruk River thirty miles south of the community of Barrow, Delbert Rexford and Marvin Kanayurak set a net under October ice.

■ **Right:** Whitefish, caught by Joe Ericklook's net in the Colville River.

Left: Steve Oomittuk and Koonukrowruk set a net in the Chukchi Sea in June on the north side of Point Hope.

go elsewhere, the Iñupiat organized the North Slope Borough under Alaska law on July 2, 1972. Nearly as large as Utah and encompassing lands north of the continental divide in the Brooks Range, the borough would give its eight tiny Iñupiat villages, whose total population numbered about five thousand, the power to levy property taxes on the pipeline, oil wells, and all other physical structures supporting the Arctic Slope oil industry.

The effort was challenged by the state of Alaska and the oil industry but upheld by the Alaska Supreme Court. Taxes were levied, bonds passed, and construction projects launched: housing, modern schools, power and sewage plants, and water projects. At the same time, the leaders of the Arctic Slope Regional Corporation formed by the settlement act launched an aggressive effort to create as many ventures as possible in the oil patch and elsewhere. Jobs and money soon began to flow into the Iñupiat villages.

Through all the change, much of it traumatic, the culture and the heart of the people remained with the bowheads. For thousands of years, Iñupiat bodies had been made and fueled by the bowheads and could not be satisfied with food that new money could buy. Iñupiaq culture remained focused on the whale, Iñupiaq communal and family ties were dependent on the hunt and the complex system of sharing and ceremonial celebration surrounding it. The Iñupiat turned a large portion of their new financial resources inward, toward the bowheads. More hunters outfitted crews.

In 1973 the National Marine Fisheries Service stationed scientists at the ice edge and began to gather biological data on the bowheads. The fisheries service concluded in 1977 that the western Arctic bowhead population numbered as few as six hundred animals and no more than eighteen hundred. The agency observed that the recovering population of Eskimo whalers was growing in size, putting out more crews and striking more bowheads. They reported this to the International Whaling Commission (IWC).

Fearing the whale population would crash beyond recovery, the commission imposed a moratorium on the ancient hunt, decreeing that in 1978 no bowhead could be hunted. The United States committed itself to enforce the moratorium, but the shocked Native whalers fought back. Their observations told them the bowhead population numbered many thousand. Drawing largely upon the financial resources of the borough, they formed the Alaska Eskimo Whaling Commission, which carried the fight to save their way of life to IWC meetings around the globe. As a result, the IWC and the United States backed off the total moratorium and established a quota, to be divided among ten whaling villages spread out over fifteen hundred miles of Alaska coastline.

The quota allowed eighteen whales to be struck by harpoon or twelve to be landed, whichever number was reached first. Typically about half the whales struck were lost, which meant the ten villages would likely wind up with as few as nine whales. In the 1977 spring season, Simon Koonook's village of Point Hope alone had landed twelve whales.

No one in the IWC or the U.S. government believed that the observations on the bowhead population by Eskimo hunters could possibly be superior to the data gathered by scientists. Still, officials agreed to further census and research efforts. The Alaska Eskimo Whaling Commission entered into an agreement with the National Oceanic and Atmospheric Administration: The Eskimo commission would live by the quota and manage and enforce it upon its own members. In exchange, the government agreed to a new, decadelong census and research program, with frequent follow-up thereafter. The goal was not only to establish a better bowhead population estimate, but also to determine if the population was growing and, if so, by how much. Studies would also determine the subsistence and cultural needs of the whaling communities for bowheads. Each year, new information and the methodology behind it would be presented to the skeptical scientific committee of the IWC. Should the data warrant, quota numbers would be reconsidered.

Right: Simon Koonook (at left) lifts his head from the theodolite to watch a bowhead pass by the whale census camp as a non-Native census-taker looks on.

While the research would be overseen by the National Marine Fisheries Service and would involve other government agencies as well as private industry, the bulk of the census and biological work would be spearheaded by the Alaska Eskimo Whaling Commission and the North Slope Borough.

In time, studies and household surveys undertaken by anthropologist Stephen Braund for the Department of the Interior would show that 97 percent of the Alaska Natives living in the studied whaling communities shared bowhead meat and maktak. Ninety-eight percent preferred wild food to store-bought meat, and more than 82 percent ate subsistence meats at least five days a week. Braund found that "neither store-bought meat nor any one species or combination of wildlife resources was a practical substitute for the bowhead whale." His studies would ultimately determine in 1977 a need for fifty-six landed bowheads each year.

Numbers do not speak of the communal and spiritual value of the hunt, however. Numbers say nothing of the relationship the people feel with the whale, nor of the values that bind together communities undertaking so huge an

Left: Concealing himself and his snowmachine behind a white blind, Billy Adams searches for seals as he slowly traverses the March ice off Barrow.

Right: After firing at a seal, Billy sprints toward the hole into which it disappeared, hoping that if he hit it, he can recover the seal before it sinks.

effort. A captain spends thousands of dollars outfitting and maintaining a crew. The entire community helps him land and butcher his bowhead. He does not sell its flesh. Except for that small part he keeps for himself and his immediate family, he gives it away. The meat is spread not only throughout the ten whaling villages, but also to other Native communities not situated to hunt bowheads, and to friends, relatives, students, and soldiers all over Alaska, the nation, and the world. The bowheads nourish not only bodies, but spirits as well.

Recent estimates indicate a population of eight thousand bowheads that migrate through Alaska's arctic waters, a figure the International Whaling Commission now accepts. The data also show a bowhead population well able to sustain a healthy harvest by the Eskimos of Alaska. The quota for the ten villages has risen correspondingly, to 255 landed whales over a five-year period—an average of fifty-one a year—with an average of sixty-seven strikes available. The efficiency of the hunters has also improved. The ratio of struck whales landed has

■ **Above:** Billy peers into the hole, looking for the seal.

■ **Right:** Billy prepares to load an *ugruk* (bearded seal) onto his sled for the trip home. Ugruks are prized both for the excellent quality of their meat and for their hides, which are used for covering skin boats and other purposes.

climbed to nearly 75 percent. Factoring in this hunt, the bowhead population is estimated to be growing at 3.1 percent annually.

During my visit to the whale census camp near Barrow in 1982, these numbers were not yet scientifically known. The quota had risen to just fifteen landed or twenty-one struck whales. Barrow's share that year was four landed or five struck. Anthropologist Braund would later demonstrate that Barrow had a need for at least fifteen whales that year.

The hunt had begun just days before my arrival on May 2 but was already over. There would be no bowheads in Barrow in 1982.

As a proxy for the outside world, I was greeted with frustration and anger.

"What would you think if we came down to your country and told you you could only kill five cows, or five chickens?" a woman scolded me. "My parents can't eat a diet of just white man's food. Sure, we like some of it now and then. But when we eat it all the time? My parents get sick. I get sick. This is what you are forcing on us." She told me of her experience at boarding school, where she was deprived of whale. "The food was not filling. I got skinny, pale, sickly. We'll be sick around here this winter, without whales."

"A whale gives himself to a person that they feel deserves them. It's not the Iñupiat way to say

you are going to get so many whales. You cannot put a number on it," whaling captain Percy Nusunginya told me.

"What this is, is extermination of a culture, without firing a shot," George Ahmaogak fumed.

The quota had caused much dissension in the community. Some wanted to defy it; to show the IWC, America, and the world that the Iñupiat hunted by his own law and no one else's. Others vowed to stick to the agreement, to prove to the world that the bowhead population was strong and to demonstrate that the Iñupiat were responsible hunters, capable of managing their own hunt within U.S. law. No matter how painful, Eskimo whaling commissioners counseled hunters to "honor the quota."

"It hurts," whaling captain and Borough Mayor Eugene Brower said of the dissension. "There's an old saying: You don't squabble over the bowhead whale. Whales sometimes send runners to check what's going on in the village. We have to be humble before this great animal." Eugene believed the hard feelings could well explain why no whales had given themselves to Barrow that spring.

A significant portion of my life had unfolded in the Lower 48 on American Indian reservations, including those of the Lakota of the Northern Plains, where few buffalo still roamed. These great animals had been slaughtered almost to extinction in what many Americans of the

Left: Walrus on an ice flow off Barrow in July.

nineteenth century considered a noble cause: depriving the Lakota access to the primary source of their physical, cultural, and spiritual survival so that they might be subdued by the United States.

I had witnessed firsthand the depth and persistence of the resultant pain. Would the Iñupiat now be deprived of the primary source of their physical, cultural, and spiritual strength to advance what many now see as a noble cause: preventing the killing of whales?

I returned to Barrow in May 1985 on a freelance assignment for *We Alaskans,* the Sunday magazine of the *Anchorage Daily News.* That fall, I contracted with the borough to publish a small pictorial magazine, which I named *The Open Lead,* in honor of that break in the ice where bowheads swim. George Ahmaogak's wife, Maggie, soon corrected me. The right word for an open lead was *uiñiq.* I then called the magazine *Uiñiq.* Most of the photos in this book originally appeared there. While it had been the bowhead that first attracted me to the Arctic, I joined the Iñupiat in significant encounters with two other species of whale: beluga and gray.

In so harsh an environment, people and creature alike continually wander into trouble. I covered several search-and-rescue operations. The most intense of all was the Iñupiat effort to seek out and rescue their own culture from the forces of a world that would destroy it.

Right: Eli Solomon searches for a bowhead whale five miles offshore from Monument, where a tall obelisk marks the site of the plane crash that killed Native American humorist Will Rogers and pioneer aviator Wiley Post.

Left: Dancers from the village of Point Hope.

ONCE THERE LIVED A MAN by the name of Katauq, an *anatkuq,* or what the English-speaking world calls a shaman. One day, as Katauq rested inside his sod iglu, others gathered there noticed that he sat perfectly still, not moving a muscle. He did not blink, nor move his head. He was breathing, and that was it. This did not worry them, for they knew that he had gone traveling. They would just let him be until his spirit returned to his body.

The spirit of Katauq traveled far, finally arriving at a great gathering of bowhead whales. They gave him a parka. When Katauq put it on, he took on the appearance of a whale, although his mind remained that of a man. Katauq spent the winter with the bowheads, living and eating as they did. He learned their habits and came to understand their ways.

As spring neared, the bowheads prepared for their journey north and east, when they would travel from what is now called the Bering Sea through the Bering Strait, into the Chukchi Sea and finally the Beaufort Sea. Along the way, the bowheads told Katauq, they would meet hunters waiting with their *umiaks,* their skin-covered boats. Some of the boats would appear light and clean, pleasing to the eye; others would be dark and dirty. If Katauq wished to give himself to a whaling crew, he must surface by a clean umiak. These belonged to respectful people; people who were considerate of others, who shared their catch with widows, orphans, the old, and all those who could not hunt for themselves. They were honest. They treated other people, and all animals, with respect.

The wives of the captains of such boats made certain that their ice cellars had been cleaned. Once the hunters removed the parka from a bowhead, it was comforting for the whale to know they would put it in a clean ice cellar.

These were the hunters to whom whales wanted to give themselves.

The dark, dirty umiaks belonged to selfish people who did not share their catch; lazy people who would not help those in need.

No whale wanted to give itself to such hunters.

Katauq paid strict attention to all that the whales taught him. They told him they had brought his spirit there so he could teach what he learned to the other hunters, who would then know to always be respectful. Katauq was told he could stay a whale and travel with them. If he should give himself to an umiak, his spirit would not die, but would return to put on another parka, as did the spirits of all bowheads received by hunters. His human body, however, would die. He would live with the whales forever, though sometimes he might be a seal, a beluga, or maybe a walrus. If Katauq wanted to return to the people of Tikiaq, Point Hope, it would be necessary for him to fly away as a duck.

Katauq began the journey with the whales. When they neared Tikiaq, he left the whales, became a king eider duck, and flew away. While the people slept, he landed near the village and returned to his human form.

Katauq told the people of his journey and of the things he had learned, and so even today, hunters know they must respect and honor the whale if they are to receive its gifts.

(The above is a condensed version of an Iñupiat story, told to me by Ernie Frankson, a Point Hope whaling captain and oral historian.)

Right: Prior to moving onto the ice to begin the spring whale hunt, a Wainwright whaling crew led by Ben Ahmaogak Sr. pauses as village elder David Kagak (right) offers a blessing upon the whalers and the bowhead they seek.

"The feeling
I get in whaling,
it's something
I'm very proud
of. Whaling has
been our way for
centuries, for
thousands and
thousands of years.
I hope it goes on
like that, without
stopping."

—CAPTAIN BEN ITTA

"GET UP!" A rough hand shook my boot, jarring me from a cold sleep. "We've got to move! Now!" It was George Ahmaogak, the whaling captain. "Get up! We can't wait for you!"

It had been a sleep with no blankets, no sleeping bag, no pillow. The kind of sleep where some parts of you manage to find warmth, others stay cool, and still others get downright cold; where you continually shift your position to warm the cold parts, only to chill the warm. Despite my Sorrel boots, all warmth had long ago fled my feet, leaving instead a pain just above numbness, a pain that deteriorated the heating capabilities of my entire body.

Still, it had been sleep, and I did not want to leave it.

"Move!"

I stumbled clumsily upward and into the painful brightness outside the tent.

Glaring sunlight reflected off a white world of ice, torn, shattered, and piled by the forces of wind and current. Tall pressure ridges rose from a broken plain of sea ice. In front of the tent the umiak sat facing a broad lead of open water that separated the ever-moving polar pack from the shore-fast ice on which we were camped—though as I soon found out, "shore-fast" is only a fleeting term.

Gloved hands of hunters, bundled in fur parkas covered with the white cotton hunting shirts that serve as camouflage, grabbed the umiak. Hurriedly they dragged the skin boat back from the water, in which we all longed to see whales.

"Don't just stand there looking," George scolded me. "Get packing! There is no time to waste!"

Already the grub boxes were being hauled from the tent, and the harpoon and darting gun were being disassembled; soon they would be packed into the umiak or onto sleds. Not quite certain what to do, I plunged back into the tent and began hauling out the caribou hides upon which I had been sleeping.

Although the ice and the sea looked to me to be no different than when I crawled onto those skins an hour earlier, the whalers knew things I didn't and could see things I couldn't.

The wind had shifted to the west. Pack ice a few hundred yards away was traveling in our direction. Soon it would crush and obliterate our campsite. Anyone still here would likely die.

In just minutes the entire camp disappeared. Food and provisions for a dozen men were packed and roped down onto big, heavy-duty, handmade utility sleds or into the umiak. Two sets of harpoons, darting guns, and shoulder guns were put away, along with rifles and shot-guns. The canvas windbreak had been taken down, folded, and tucked inside the umiak. The parachute over the tent was gone, as was the tent itself and all of its contents.

We were ready to go. Hunters tugged at the starter cords of their snowmachines, which one by one roared to life. Hunters without machines began to climb onto the back of sleds in prepa-ration for the ride out.

Now fully awake but still unclear as to what was happening, I began looking for a sled to ride on.

"No you don't!" George shouted upon seeing what I was doing. "You are going to *umiaruk!*"

Umiaruk? Umiak! I stumbled dazedly to the umiak and started to climb inside.

"No!" George shouted. "You don't ride in the umiak! You run with it! You hold onto it! You protect it!"

George positioned me on the right side of the umiak, which was now on a sled connected to his Ski-Doo Safari 477 by a long rope. Byron Agiak, robust and cocky, was on the other side, enjoying my stupidity. He was sixteen and had lived this way all his life. I was thirty-four, out of shape, trying to recover from bronchitis, and in an envi-ronment as alien to me as the back side of the moon.

Grinning broadly, Byron grabbed hold of the left gunwale. I copied his actions.

George squeezed the throttle; his snowmachine began to move. The rope went taut, stretched, and then with the help of a bit of rocking by Byron and myself, jerked the sled carrying the umiak free from the frozen grip of the ice and onto the trail. Byron and I began to run along-side the sled.

We encountered a pressure ridge. George gunned his machine and roared to the top. I struggled to keep my footing, let alone protect the umiak. We topped the ridge. The trail jogged to the right. Byron kept the umiak under control.

On the downslope I lost my balance and

Previous page: Jonathan Aiken Sr., known as Kunuk, sees possible danger as ice moves in on his camp from the west.

Right: An umiak made by the elder Patrick Attungana sits outside the Point Hope home of his son, Henry, awaiting a new cover of ugruk skins.

threw my weight on the umiak for support. We plummeted down the grade toward a shard of ice that threatened to poke a hole in the umiak skin—or in me. I fought to regain my balance. The umiak jerked away from the shard. I could take no credit. I kicked the shard as I passed by. Suddenly my foot plunged into a crack hidden by drifted snow. The umiak tore loose of my grasp. I flopped forward. Snow stung my face as I fell flat.

Thinking how easy one could break a leg doing this, I jerked my head up to see George driving on and looking back through dark glasses that only seemed to magnify his disgust. Another snowmachine towing a sled was scooting down the hill. I rolled out of the way. The machine passed by my head, followed by the heavy, steel-rimmed runners of the sled. I got up and chased after the umiak, my lungs burning with the effort, and managed to catch up to it. We had now reached a flat stretch, but another pressure ridge loomed a short distance ahead.

Supporting as much of my weight as possible on the gunwale, I flopped awkwardly along,

Previous page: Convinced that advancing ice threatens the hunters' safety, Kunuk gives the order to abandon camp.

Left: On another day, the ice breaks on the shore side of camp. Kunuk's crew rushes to strike camp and get across the ice before it becomes too wide for their snow-machines.

Right: A hunter protects the umiak belonging to George Ahmaogak as his crew flees advancing ice.

struggling to recover my breath. Sweat soaked my clothing. The snow would be hard under my feet, then suddenly soft, and I would sink knee-deep and have to kick my way out.

As we passed through the next pressure ridge, the umiak careened off the trail. I could not stop it. Radiating disgust, Byron jerked the umiak back onto the trail. I stepped into another crack. Again I fell. Again I got up. Again I ran after and caught the umiak.

When I fell on another pressure ridge, George stopped. Breathing fire, he came stomping back toward me.

"You don't grab the boat here," he said, motioning to the thin framework I gripped. "You might break it yourself, doing that. You grab it here." He took hold of a sturdy beam. "And you don't run like this!" With a silly smile on his face, he jogged in place in a mocking fashion, one hand timidly holding on and the other flopping about like a broken wing on a chicken.

"You run like this!" He imitated a deliberate, confident jog. "And when there is a bump, you brace like this." He pulled up on the gunwale, flexing his legs to take the shock. "You are a shock absorber. A human shock absorber." George stormed back to his snowmachine, jerked on the cord, and we were off again.

Up one pressure ridge, then down another, we clambered over broken ice. My arms, chest, and back strained with each blow. I pushed around a protruding shard and again stuck my foot in a crack and plunged headlong into the snow. With my lungs burning, sweat stinging my eyes, and wet hair sticking to my forehead, I struggled to my feet, fell again, and had to get up and catch the boat again.

I don't know how long this went on, but finally I could run no more. I decided I would just flop down in the snow and quit.

Then I pictured myself, a weak white man, lying collapsed on the ice while the Iñupiat passed by, laughing with disdain. I did not let go. I kept running . . . and running . . . and running.

Inevitably I hit a point of absolute exhaustion. Forcing myself, I took one more step, then prepared to collapse. Somehow I found still another step, one more, and then I had nothing left. But before I could fall, George stopped and killed his machine. We had reached safe ice. My lungs struggled for air. My stomach fought to hold onto its contents, but could not. I gasped, coughed, and retched, then did it again.

Through teary eyes, I could see the blurry image of George studying me. He began to laugh. Anger grew in me, causing me to convulse even more violently. George laughed harder. All the whalers were laughing, laughing at the *Taniq*, the white man, retching his guts out in the middle of a sea of broken ice. Laughing loudest of all was the captain.

I wanted to damage the man. My brain

Left: Kunuk's crew races to cross over a widening crack in the ice.

shouted obscenities, but my lips and lungs could not hurl them.

Then through my bleary vision I detected a friendly glow in the captain's eyes. This was not a malicious laugh. It was not derision. It was the laugh of goodwill and fellowship, a laugh that said, "We put you to the test, and you passed—not gracefully, but you passed."

I started to laugh. They laughed even louder. This made me laugh harder still. It hurt terribly, to laugh in that condition. Still, it was good to laugh.

Days earlier, I had come to Barrow to do a profile on the new mayor for *We Alaskans.* I had followed a suit-clad George Ahmaogak about as he met with bankers, oil executives, and staff. He did this work in a courteous, professional manner, yet whenever we would break away, he would grumble, "I can't wait to get out of this damn suit, onto my Ski-Doo, and out to the whales." Finally he replaced his suit and tie with a white hunting parka. In it, he looked more like himself—ruggedly handsome, charismatic, and self-assured. His three-year-old daughter, Eda Lee, tried to block our departure through the door. She wept angry tears, convinced this would soften her father's heart and persuade him to take her to whale camp.

She was wrong.

George mounted his snowmachine. I climbed on behind him.

The trail to camp wrapped and twisted its way inside a maze of mountainous pressure ridges, which would take us a full hour to thread our way through. We would traverse close to fifteen miles of trail to get to a camp pitched on the ice about five miles offshore.

A snowmachine is great when you are in the driver's seat, the pivot point. If the trail is reasonably smooth, the backseat is not so bad. If the trail traverses rough ice, however, and your pack is filled with camera gear and strapped to your shoulders, throwing off your center of gravity, riding the back of a snowmachine is like being perched on the end of a teeter-totter gone mad. The force of every bump is leveraged into your rear end, alternately threatening to hurtle you into giant shards of ice or to crush your spine.

At each turn and bump, I was convinced I was about to be bucked off. Somehow I would manage to stay on.

"You okay?" George would holler.

"Yea!" I would shout. "Fine."

I discovered that by taking my feet off the rail and suspending them at a certain angle from the machine, I could mitigate the unbalancing effect of the backpack.

"Keep your feet on the rails!" George shouted angrily upon discovering my new technique. "Never take them off! You'll rip your damn legs off!"

Right: Hunters help push a sled loaded with bowhead meat through a series of pressure ridges on the ice.

The temperature was somewhere between zero and ten below, less whatever windchill we were generating. Yet I worked so hard just to stay on the snowmachine, I was soon drenched in sweat.

George and his brother, Lawrence, better known as Savik, meaning knife, alternated as whaling crew captains. Officially this was Savik's year. Unfortunately he had broken both legs the summer before while being blanket-tossed fifteen feet into the air in celebration of a bowhead

taken by another crew of Ahmaogak's, living in Wainwright. Savik's legs were still too weak for the rigors of camp life. George was in charge.

It was late evening. The sun cruised low over the icy horizon to the northwest. Although we were still a few days from the last sunset of the season, we had entered the time of year when there is no darkness. Sunset would slowly give way to a couple of hours of pastel blue twilight, which would then yield to the glow of sunrise.

Left: A polar bear approaches a group of whalers, looking them straight in the eye. Unlike most arctic animals, polar bears generally show no fear of men.

Right: Larry Itta keeps his rifle leveled at one of seven polar bears that seek to invade the Ahmaogak camp. Other hunters fire into the air, yell, and rev their snowmachines. At the last possible moment, the bear turns to leave, as do five of the others.

Left: The seventh bear would not turn away, so it was either the bear or a hunter.

A nearly full moon hung over the parachute-draped wall tent as we pulled into camp. The tent sat on thick, multiyear ice anchored fast to the shore. In front of this stretched a broad plain of thin, new ice, covering what should have been open water at this time of year. This new ice reached out about half a mile to the polar pack—the constantly drifting, moving, cracking layer of ice wrapped over the North Pole, stretching from Alaska to the far reaches of Russia, Finland, and Greenland.

In front of the tent, pointed seaward, sat the umiak. A harpoon and darting gun, carefully positioned at the bow, stood ready. A bright orange float, covered with canvas, sat a short distance behind the harpoon. Beneath the canvas, a heavy rope was coiled neatly around the top of the float. From there it ran to the fore of the umiak, where it was wrapped in another meticulous coil, out of which it emerged to attach to the harpoon. On both sides of the umiak, flat slabs of ice stood upright, like ragged tombstones. When the lead opened, these would serve as a blind to conceal hunters from migrating whales.

Behind and to the right of the umiak, a sled resting on two blocks of ice was being used as a bench. A canvas windbreak was in place behind the sled. A battery of rifles and shotguns stood ready just off the windbreak—not for whales, but for seals and ducks, and for protection against polar bears. Two hunters sat on the bench. Always, twenty-four hours a day, lead open or closed, hunters would be sitting on the bench, leaning against the boat, or climbing atop nearby ice peaks. If the lead opened and whales appeared, the hunters wanted to know immediately. If wind and currents turned unfavorable and icebergs moved in from the pack to threaten the campsite, they wanted to know. If the ice broke behind the camp and began drifting to sea, they wanted to know.

Anything that could be seen from the water was white—the tent, the parachute covering it, the umiak, and the parkas worn by the hunters. The many-hued snowmachines were parked far enough back from where the water was expected to open that no passing whale could see them. I wore a green, down-filled parka, a white man's parka, the kind the oil-field workers wear. I was given a white hunting shirt to put over it. I would soon discover that while the down parka was great for keeping me reasonably warm for a day or two, after continuous use and wear it lost its insulation value, causing my quality of life to deteriorate rapidly. Not so with the fur parkas worn by the hunters.

George took me inside the tent, which was set up in the basic manner of every whaling tent I have been in since. Just inside the door, to the left, was a big, homemade wooden grub box; next to that, a large picnic-type ice chest that protected the food within from freezing. A tall antenna attached to the CB radio was lashed to the front tent pole and reached high above it.

In front of the radio, a kerosene stove burned. Sitting atop it, a big pan contained melting freshwater ice. To the right, coffee and tea simmered over the blue flame of a Coleman stove. Nearby stood a pile of dishes and cookware, dirty from dinner. Just past the grub and cooking area, several caribou hides and one brown-bear skin had been piled on a floor made of large slabs of Styrofoam over which quarter-inch plywood sheets had been laid. Atop these furs lay a sleeping Perry Okpeaha, still wearing his insulated pants and boots, ready to leap into instant action should the need arise. Several more hunters, ranging in age from sixteen to about fifty-five, lounged around on the caribou hides or sat on the grub box.

One was a slender, wild-looking fellow with a boisterous laugh, who immediately sought to make me feel comfortable, and whom I immediately liked. This was Glenn Roy Edwards. Another was Savik's son, Roy, friendly from the first moment. Still stung by the recent International Whaling Commission quota and skeptical of outsiders, most of the other hunters greeted me with cordial coolness, while the oldest radiated outright mistrust. It was clear he did not want me in the camp, but if his captain, George, did, he would tolerate me.

Years would pass before this man showed me a sign of friendship or warmth. This happened one night after I threw aside my terrible shyness, put down my cameras, stepped out onto the dance floor, and stomped about in an awkward attempt to match the powerful beat of a dozen skin drums, one of which was held by this hunter. When I walked off the floor, his eyes twinkled happily and a smile warmed his rugged face. "All right!" he said, patting my shoulder. From that moment until his death, he would treat me with warmth and respect.

But back in that tent, however, the kindest consideration he could show me was to act as though I were not there. He pulled out a deck of cards and a cribbage board and struck up a game. Glenn Roy bowed out, choosing not to play and to leave the tent entirely. "I haven't played in a long time. I wouldn't do so good," he apologized lamely as he pushed the flap aside and stepped out.

Feeling awkward and uncomfortable, I followed him. We sat on the sled bench, drinking Pepsi. Glenn Roy began telling me about different guns he had owned, or wanted, or had had repaired, and how much it had all cost, or would have cost if he could have afforded it. I don't remember the particulars, but feeling lonely and lost, I was glad to have someone talking to me like maybe I already knew something.

"I wonder what the current is doing," Glenn Roy said after a while. "There's no wind. We

Right: Itta approaches the downed bear with caution, though it died instantly.

need some current to move this new ice out and give us an open lead. We've got whales to hunt! We need some current!" He left the bench and squatted in front of the umiak. Curious, I followed him. The sun was down now. The moon grew brighter in the pastel sky, and the light falling over the ice was softly hued. Just in front of the boat, a tiny hole had been cut in the new ice, which was only about an inch thick.

Removing the glove from his right hand, Glenn Roy scooped slush from the hole, then shoved his empty Pepsi can into the water. It filled quickly, then tipped upside down. The bottom shone silver in the twilight. As the can sank, the aluminum bottom cast an eerie glow. It sank straight down, into shockingly clear water. Two feet. Five feet. Ten, fifteen, twenty, twenty-five, thirty feet. Finally it disappeared, too tiny to be seen any longer.

"Well, there's no current," Glenn Roy muttered, "We won't be seeing any open water for a while. No whales, either."

Getting chilled, I stepped back into the tent. The cribbage game was coming to an end. George had teamed up with Fred Okpeaha. They had lost. "Out!" George pointed to the tent flap, roaring with feigned anger. This command was not directed at me, but at the cardplayers who had beaten him. Laughing, the victorious cribbage players tumbled through the flaps into the subzero air outside. I followed. "Now you see

why I never play cribbage," Glenn Roy said with a chuckle. As the price of their defeat, George and Fred now had to wash and dry the dishes and thoroughly clean up the inside of the tent.

I was also glad I hadn't played. This pleasure would be short-lived, however. Young whale hunters begin their education on the ice performing housekeeping tasks. George had done so, as had Fred, Glenn Roy, and every person out there but me. Just because I was a visiting Taniq photographer and no longer a teenager didn't mean I was going to get out of it.

The next morning, I began a regimen of washing dishes, keeping a pot of coffee brewed—hot and fresh at all times—along with another of tea. I had to see that everything was in its place. If I did not know how to do something, no one would tell me. The learning process was to figure it out for myself. When I was told to chop freshwater ice to melt for coffee, I was perplexed. How was I to find freshwater ice five miles out on the ocean? No one volunteered the information. Yet eventually I observed a nearby quarry where ice had been extracted from a patch of rounded-off, smooth, bluish ice. This was old ice that been lifted above sea level and suspended in the elements for so long that the salt had leached out of it. This was the camp supply of fresh water.

George insisted on a clean and well-organized camp. He would suffer nothing being **out of**

Left: "Tanngassksiruq inna!" Seventy-six-year-old Roxy Oyagak had happily greeted another hunter clad in a white parka, who was approaching on the ice directly in front of him. But the other hunter had answered with only a silent stare. Squinting from behind his thick glasses, Roxy realized this hunter was actually *nanuq*, and he was its prey. Quickly, Roxy raised and fired his rifle. He then brought the bear home to his family.

place, nor would he tolerate clutter of any kind. Not only would a sloppy camp slow down hunters in need of quick relocation, it could also cost them a bowhead. One day I carelessly laid some just-washed pans in the pathway to the tent door. My reprimand came quickly. "Whales do not want to give themselves to crews who keep sloppy camps," George admonished. "When a whale comes by, it's going to be looking, smelling, and listening. Someone's going to kick this pot over, its going to hear it, and we're never going to see that whale again."

Once I strolled about thirty feet to the left of the tent, where I stood and watched the snow in front of me turn yellow. "Bill!" I heard an angry voice yell. "Don't you know better yet than to piss on the left side of the tent?" Left is the down-lead side, the direction from which a whale would approach. It was too late, I couldn't stop. I heard a few snickers from other whalers. I quickly learned to go to the right.

After the dishes were washed and dried that

Left: Women gather in the home of whaling captain Eugene Brower to sew seven ugruk hides into the single skin that will cover his umiak.

Right: In Point Hope, Ella Lisbourne helps sew the cover for Henry Attungana's umiak.

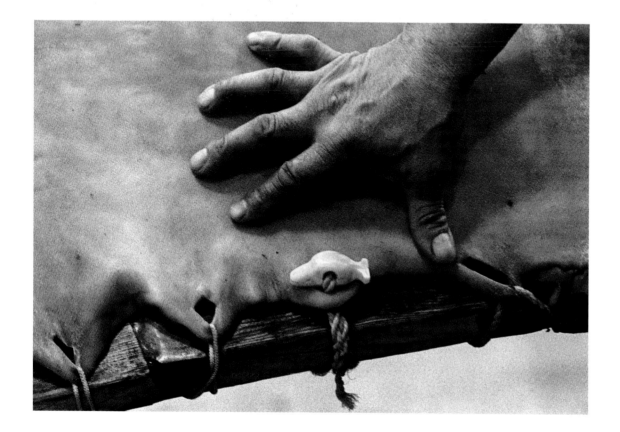

first night, the camp was cleaned and fresh coffee was brewed for those on watch. The rest of us squeezed together on top of the caribou skins. Everyone quickly fell asleep—except for me. I was too excited. I spent the entire night lying awake, listening to the constant chatter on the CB radio. Considerable conversation took place between the residents of different camps and the family and crew members at the home "base camps" in town. Voices had started saying good night as early as midnight, and others kept saying

good night until about 4:00 A.M., when they started saying, "Good morning, good morning, good morning, everybody."

This kept up until about 10:00 A.M., by which time just about everyone who had slept during the night was up and about, and those on night shift were sleeping. Many conversations traveled the radio waves that night, discussing ice conditions, weather, and whale sightings to the south. Many conversations were totally in Iñupiaq, which I couldn't understand. Many were a mixture of English and Inupiaq. Others took place entirely in English. Sometimes Asian voices, unintelligible to any of us and coming from who knew where, scratched their way through the radio.

The actual words of only one conversation remained clearly implanted in my brain, perhaps because I was so far from my own four children. It began with the tiny voice of a boy back in town who had just made contact with a father he dearly missed, a father whom the boy was eager to follow on the whale hunt, if only he were older.

"How's my dad?" the boy asked his father.
"Fine."
"See any whales yet?"
"No. No water."
"How far are you from Jacob's camp?" the little voice asked.
"About one mile," the big voice crackled back. "We're going to have to clear the airwaves now. Maybe this ice will open and whales will come."
"Good-bye," the little voice yielded, longingly. "Love you!"
"Love you, too."

By the middle of the next day, Mother Nature still showed no signs of clearing out the thin ice covering the lead.

"There's lots of roadwork to do," George announced. "We've got some time, let's make good use of it. We can cut a shortcut through that pressure ridge right over there." He pointed to a virgin mountain range of ice to the south-east. Grabbing pickaxes, regular axes, and long poles with half-moon–shaped knives attached to them, the hunters went to work. Anticipating that sleds heavily laden with bowheads might

Left: More than thirty years ago, whaling captain Amos Lane gave this ivory whale talisman to Patrick Attungana, who faithfully attached it to each new umiak skin covering. After taking over whaling responsibilities from his father, Henry Attungana did the same.

Right: After chopping, melting, and brewing fresh-water ice into coffee, apprentice hunter Qayan Harcharek cradles the product of his labor in his arms.

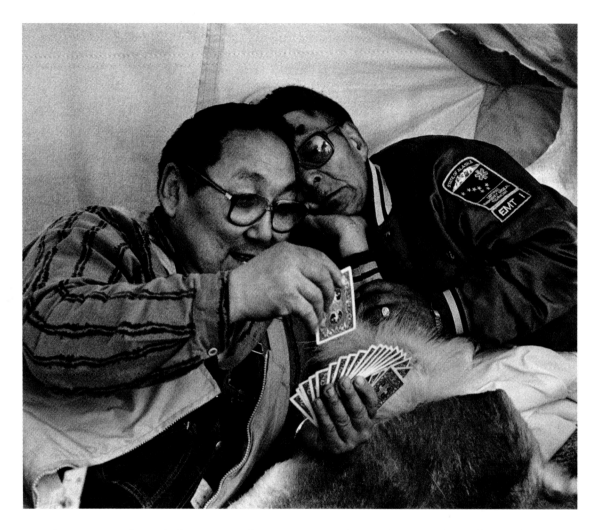

soon be traversing the trail, George wanted it to be as smooth as possible.

They looked for the lowest place in the ridge, to serve as a pass. Using pickaxes and the other tools, they set to breaking large, jagged shards into pieces. Holes were filled with chunks of ice. High barriers were knocked down. Then they moved on to the next ridge and began the process all over again.

Just about the time I was starting to figure out how to make a photograph of this scene, George looked at me with a stern scowl. "How many pictures do you need?" he scolded. "Put down your cameras, grab a pick, and help out a bit. Do

Left: During a relaxed moment when the west wind has closed the lead and the crews have relocated to safe ice, Eli Solomon peeks at the hand of Raymond Kalayuak.

Right: Byron Agiak cuts a snowmachine trail through a pressure ridge.

some work. Nobody gets away with not working in my camp! Here, take my pick."

And I did. He was, after all, the captain.

I'd see a whaler strike a large shard of ice with his pick. It would split in half, sometimes into three or four pieces. He then reduced these to rubble in short order.

I'd flail away at a similar-size chunk many times before achieving the same result. I would swing ever harder and feel ever more foolish.

Previous page: Eider ducks fly along the lead in late May as a whaling crew paddles their umiak in search of bowhead.

Left: During the first week of July, Pete Lisbourne, or Koonuknowruk, guides a boat through a floe of rotting ice toward the cliffs of Cape Thompson.

Right: Upon reaching the cliffs, Koonuknowruk and Steve Oommituk look for a good place to climb for murre eggs, as murres and seagulls take to the air.

As I kept working, the heat got to me. I took off my parka. It got worse and I took off the jacket I wore underneath. Now I had on just a long-sleeve wool shirt and a sweater. Still I was too hot. Sweat soaked my clothes.

"Here, let me take that pick for a while," Glenn Roy offered after a bit. By now, my hair

was wet; dripping sweat stung my eyes, and I could taste the salt.

"What you don't want to do out here is get all hot and sweaty. You'll freeze later, believe me," Glenn Roy counseled. "I'll do it for a while, then you can do it again." In fact, that's what all the whalers were doing. Before they could get too overheated, they would pass the pick to someone else.

The Arnold Brower crew—known as the ABC crew—joined us in building the road. The captain, Arnold Brower Sr., was staying in town, so Arnold Jr. was running the camp for his father. By my reckoning, Arnold Jr. is as skilled as any captain. Yet for as long as I have known him, he has been loyal to his elderly father's crew. He has run the camp, directed the crew, and killed the whale, but always has given the credit to his captain, his father.

"Pretty tough work," I told Arnold. "I can hardly imagine how the old-time hunters did it, when they had to come out here, with dogs, and no steel tools."

"It was no problem for them," he answered flatly. "When you come out as a group, with your family, your people, and you are working for your community, it's no problem."

Later, after the road had been built, I wandered by Arnold's camp. Crew members sat happily outside enjoying the sunshine.

"Hey, Bill," Arnold's brother Johnny shouted

Left: Koonuknowruk plucks an egg from the tiny ledge on which it was laid. Immediately after he leaves, the murre that deposited it will lay another.

Right: Koonuknowruk and his hard-won eggs, atop the cliffs of Cape Thompson.

as I approached. "You think this ice is going to open?"

"I don't know."

"Why don't you go out there and check it for us?"

I knew he was making some kind of joke on me, but I wasn't quite certain what.

"Just walk out there on that ice," he said as he motioned to the young ice, which had thickened overnight to about two inches, "and see what it's like out there. Take a pole with you. If you fall through, you can catch yourself with that pole. We'll come and get you, all right."

I had seen no one step onto the thin ice. Maybe farther out it was even thinner.

"I think I'll just stay here," I said. Johnny laughed.

A bit later, I was back at the Ahmaogak camp.

"Look at that," someone said. I turned in the direction he was gazing. There was Arnold Jr., walking about a hundred feet out, checking the condition of the thin ice. He held a long pole at his waist, like a tightrope walker. I wondered what prevented him from falling through. I would later learn that there is an elasticity to saltwater ice. A skilled hunter can cross amazingly thin stretches without falling through.

I ended my second day in a state of extreme exhaustion, thanks to my night of no sleep and my day of hard work. I removed my parka, found an unoccupied spot on the caribou skins, and collapsed face down, placing my parka on top of me.

My nose, cheeks, and eyes sank into the fur, where they found warmth. It was shortly after midnight. Although cold crept into the more unprotected parts of my body, I immediately fell asleep.

⏤

While the men waited for open water and whales, they hunted eider ducks. "Hey, Hess!" Roy Ahmaogak called to me the next day. Roy sat with Glenn Roy, Walton Ahmaogak, and Perry Okpeaha outside the tent. In front of them was a Coleman stove with a pot of boiling stew on it. "Try some of this," Roy offered. "Fresh eider soup."

The ducks had been cooked with onions, rice, and salt. It's possible that at some point in my life, I have eaten something that tasted better to me than those ducks did at that moment, but if so, I can't remember it.

I had a second bowl, and a third.

Roy was happy about that. "So, how do you like it?" he asked. In answer, I ladled out another bowl. He grinned with pleasure.

Our diet consisted of a mixture of subsistence and store-bought foods. When I first arrived at the camp, I had seen the dead and frozen body of a seal lying just outside the tent. Nearby were the hindquarters of a caribou. We ate the seal, and the caribou too. When we got down to the caribou bone, we broke it open and ate the frozen marrow, which melted on the tongue and was delicious.

Right: Vincent Nageak Jr. hunts eiders while the lead is closed.

There were always a few frozen whitefish or grayling to be munched on, and dried fish too. Improvised crab pots, attached to long ropes and lowered to the sea bottom, came up teeming with small, white snow crabs.

There was no maktak or whale meat in camp.

With so small a whale quota, even careful saving had failed to leave anything for the whalers to take to camp.

There were candy, cookies, pilot bread, spam, eggs, and bacon. Sometimes George's wife, Maggie, would cook up something special back

Left: Wainwright whalers haul gear to camp as an "ice bow" brightens the sky.

Right: The crew of George Ahmaogak; the captain steers from the stern.

in Barrow, like chicken or roast of caribou, and send it out on a sled, packed in an ice chest to keep it insulated and hot. Cases of pop would occasionally arrive but would disappear rapidly.

⸺

During a day so bright with sunshine that even dark sunglasses could not prevent the stab of pain into my eyes, a tiny crack opened in the lead. Hearing the news, sleeping hunters awoke in the tents and poured out into the cold. Everyone gathered at the edge of the crack to watch it grow: one inch, two inches; one foot, a yard. It grew slowly, but persistently. The lead was opening. Whales would be coming. To the south of us, about two hundred yards away, the hunters in the ABC crew were watching also.

The day after the ice cracked, the lead had widened to about a half mile. "I can't wait for the bowheads," George said. "They're coming soon. I can feel it."

"Watch for belugas," Glenn Roy told me, referring to the small white whales so abundant in these waters. "They like to swim just in front of bowheads. They know bowheads are smart, and so they like to travel with them. When you see belugas, you're going to see bowheads pretty quick."

Certain that whales would be coming soon, the hunters now spent few of their waking hours inside the tent.

Whalers took their positions sitting at the windbreak, leaning against the umiak, or standing precariously atop sharp, narrow peaks of broken ice, intently scanning the sea, searching for bowheads but seeing none. They were seeing eider ducks returning to their birthing grounds from winter retreats far to the south. The eiders flew by in elongated Vs, following the edge of the lead. Sometimes they flew very low, only a few feet over the water. Sometimes they traveled over the ice, at altitudes ranging from about twenty to two hundred feet. They passed by, a few dozen at a time, a few score at a time. There were hundreds of ducks, thousands of ducks, hundreds of thousands.

Millions.

When they passed close, their wings could be heard beating through the cold air, accompanied by the sound of their shrill, scolding little grunts.

In time, I grew cold. Exhaustion overcame fascination. I crawled back into the tent, fell onto the caribou skins, and waited to doze off.

"Hey, Hess!" An excited voice disrupted my nap. "You're missing the action!"

It was Roy.

I grabbed my cameras and staggered through the door behind him, forgetting my sunglasses. The light struck my eyes like a knife. At first I could see nothing. Gradually I brought into focus the world of ice, water, and sun. Sun rays streaming down onto ice and snow, and ricocheting off through layers of unevenly heated air,

Right: George Ahmaogak waits for a whale.

bent and twisted and created myriad mirages. Broken ridges of ice, leaning in all directions on the distant pack, hung in midair. Distorted and enlarged, the jagged ice took on the shapes of fairy-tale castles and battlements.

Far away, too far for the sound to reach us, somewhere in a crack in the polar pack, far beyond umiak range, a great mass of black flesh, topped by a white snout, rose raggedly into the mirage, lifted skyward, twisted half a turn, then dropped silently back into the ocean.

A bowhead.

It breached twice again, then disappeared. In my sleepy state, my vision enhanced by the rippled light, the whale seemed surreal, part of a scene from a cold, frozen dream.

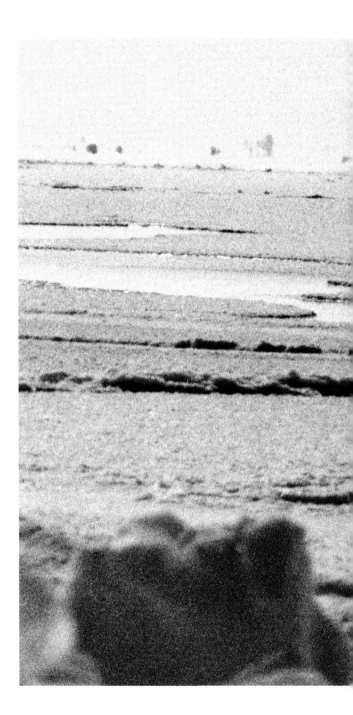

■ **Right:** Appearing as a mirage, a bowhead breaches in the distance.

"We have
followed our
fathers for decades
on, that's the way
I feel. If we lose
our whaling, then
we lose our culture.
We lose our festivals,
our Nalukataq,
Thanksgiving,
Christmas. When
that is gone, what
do we have to look
forward to?"

—Thomas Brower III

IN AUGUST, Barrow elder Gene Numnik observed some peculiar cloud formations that told him of turbulent storms soon to lash the arctic coast with destructive force.

On September 7 the rain came hard and continued overnight. Two inches poured down on Barrow, which averages only four inches annually. Early on September 8, the clouds vanished. The day turned into one of stunning clarity and exceptional warmth.

I parked a mud-spattered government Chevy pickup outside the big turquoise-colored headquarters of the North Slope Borough and went inside to find Arnold Brower Jr., special assistant to the mayor and chairman of the Alaska Eskimo Whaling Commission. Arnold wanted my help on an AEWC brochure. But before we could get down to business, one of the mayor's secretaries, Eileen Boskovsky, interrupted us.

"They just found some more frozen bodies," she said. "Down by the ocean, in front of the old Polar Bear Day Care Center. There's already a crowd of people gathering down there."

I bolted down the stairs, jumped into the truck, drove through the mud, and finally parked a ways back from the low permafrost bluff standing between the day-care center and the Chukchi Sea.

"You looking for the body?" a woman asked. "Follow me."

She led me down the descending bluff edge to where it rose just a few feet over the pebble beach. I jumped off, then followed the beach back alongside the bluff.

The overnight torrent had saturated the old face of the silt and ice bluff and caused it to collapse. A small but growing gathering of people stared intently at a point about ten to twelve feet up the newly uncovered face of the bluff, less than three feet from the top.

Protruding from a slab of sod-covered ice was a muddy mukluk, with a foot in it, heel up, indicating that the attached body was lying face down in the permafrost. The mukluk appeared to be made of caribou skin, bound to the foot by leather thongs, with seal-skin soles. Beneath the foot was what appeared to be a mat of bowhead baleen. Strands of baleen had slid down the bluff face; others protruded outward. Also protruding from the permafrost was a pouch and what looked to be the shaft of a spear or harpoon. Alongside this was the flipper of a seal and beyond that another bag that appeared to be a seal poke full of something—judging from the pungent aroma, I would have guessed rancid seal oil. Tiny bones of eider ducks and geese were scattered about, as were larger bones from caribou and fox. In front of where the person's head lay buried was the rib bone of a bowhead whale. Olaf Okpeaha had discovered the foot and the other objects during a late-morning walk.

A young father picked up a slab of baleen from the beach, then crouched beside his daughter of about two years. A long-dead whale had used

■ **Previous page:** Charlie Brower stretches his arms above the body of "Uncle Foot" lying in the permafrost atop a bed of ancient bowhead baleen.

■ **Left:** Mayor George Ahmaogak studies the visitor from the old-time as onlookers gather around.

this baleen, a natural plastic called keratin, to strain plankton and small crustaceans from the sea. As many as 360 of the fringed baleen plates, growing to fourteen feet in length, can be found in the cavernous mouth of a bowhead. No longer black and shiny, the slab had faded into a mottled brown. The father peeled back a layer from it, then held it up to the sky for his fascinated daughter to admire. It glowed as sun rays traveled through it.

High school senior Nedra Nusunginya gazed intently up at the foot with a look of fascination, oblivious to all else. Her younger brother, John, stepped to my side. "I used to play right over this," he mused. "Me and my friends would run all over here. Right here! It was fun! We never thought of anything like this being here."

To most observers, the foot in the mukluk looked to be that of a full-grown man. To John, the foot seemed small. "I think it's a boy. Maybe thirteen. He probably used to run around here, play, and have a good time, like me and my friends did." John fell silent, studying the foot in wonder. A bit of flesh was visible in a small gap separating the mukluk from the pant leg. The flesh looked like the painted skin of a mannequin.

"Maybe he was my old-time," John said softly. Perhaps the body and John were genetically connected. Perhaps, in Iñupiaq, John even carried his name and spirit.

Many of those gathered were expounding on

their observations, taking obvious pleasure in their ability to recognize so many items in what appeared to be a destroyed house, perhaps built before the voyage of Columbus.

"This was the door to the house over here," a hunter observed, "where that whalebone is."

"See that seal, there?" another said, pointing to the flipper. "Just like we have."

Because this was municipal reserve land, Earl Finkler, Barrow city manager and KBRW sportscaster and commentator, had come to represent the city's interest. Earl is a tall, lanky, well-liked white guy with a narrow face and mustache, dark hair, and a goofy sense of humor.

"Looks like that guy is pretty big," someone said. "Hey Earl, why don't you go up there and put your leg next to his, so we can compare how big he is?" Laughter rippled throughout the crowd.

Until the mayor, George Ahmaogak, could arrive, Ronald Brower, chairman of the Iñupiat History, Language, and Culture Commission, had assumed the role of person in charge. He climbed carefully up the muddy slope of the bluff, reached out, touched the foot, then remembered how, as a child, he had been counseled by elders never to touch a corpse released from the permafrost. Back then he had touched one anyway. Shortly thereafter, Barrow had been devastated by the worst storm in modern times.

Two years before the foot appeared, just a few hundred yards away, House Mound 44 had been

similarly exposed and, with the consent and guidance of the Iñupiat elders, subsequently excavated. Iñupiat high school students helped in the work. Two frozen and perfectly preserved female bodies had been found, along with three skeletons and many artifacts. Much of value had been learned. An autopsy revealed that one of the women was an elder who had long suffered from a severe, debilitating illness. Yet she had evidently been well cared for—this in the face of popular notions that it was the way of the Iñupiat to put their sick and elderly out into the cold, to die. After the autopsies the modern elders saw to it that their ancestors were honored with a proper funeral and burial.

It was determined that in the sixteenth century the people in House Mound 44 had been going about their usual business in their sod iglu, doubtless grateful for the shelter it offered against the fierce winds that must have been blowing. Without warning, a great sheet of ice surged in from the sea and charged swiftly up the beach. Another sheet slid up over the top of that, another over that, until finally a killing slab of ice climbed up over the bluff, rose over the iglu, and collapsed upon it, killing those inside.

Speculation now held that the man in the ice may have been killed by the same *ivu* (the massing of ice on shore). The only way to know for certain would be to conduct another archaeological excavation. Earl, Ronald, and George, as well

as the coroner, the public works director, and a scientist from the borough's Wildlife Management Department, gathered to discuss options.

All agreed that the site should be carefully excavated, under the oversight of the Iñupiat elders, before it eroded away. Whatever secrets of the Iñupiat past that could be unlocked here would be made available to the school children of today. The temperature pushed fifty. This was unusual and fleeting warmth and would soon be driven out of the north country. A careful archaeological dig of the site would take at least one month. In much less time, Barrow would be hard-locked into its annual nine-month deep freeze.

However momentary the warmth, it could cause premature thawing and rot to set in. More rain could further erode the bluff. One option was to tear the body out of the permafrost, conduct an autopsy, hold a funeral, then come back the next summer to excavate the site. Such a hurried body removal could damage the site, however. Valuable information would be lost forever.

Johnny Aiken, eldest son of whaling captain Jonathan Aiken Sr., stood suddenly at my side, nudging me. "It looks like he eats the same food we eat," he observed solemnly.

I looked at the foot and the artifacts. I thought of the time I had spent on the ice, following hunters in pursuit of the same animals whose bones lay here. We had amenities this man had never imagined. When conditions made the ice

Left: The same storms that exposed Uncle Foot caused the permafrost bluff to completely separate from the mainland a short distance down the coast.

too dangerous a place to be, we had beat quick retreats on snowmachines to heated buildings, warm beds, and hot showers.

And it had been tough.

Scattered about the foot were remains of the same animals I had followed the hunters in pursuit of, but none of the guns, Coleman stoves, snowmachines, and other modern items that we now looked at as necessities.

Standing in the warm sun, I shivered at the thought of what the man encased in the ice above me had endured.

How tough he must have been!

It was agreed. An immediate effort would be launched to cover and insulate the site from the temporary heat wave. Winter would soon set in, and nature would keep the site preserved until next summer, when a careful body removal and excavation could take place. Ronald placed a call to Fairbanks archaeologist Jack Lobdell, who had headed up the House Mound 44 excavation. Jack would soon jet to Barrow.

The milling crowd transformed itself into crews of busy people. Police officers cordoned off the area at the top of the bluff with bright yellow tape. Half a dozen National Guardsmen showed up, dressed in summer camouflage, and took up posts atop the bluff, planning to protect the site until freeze-up. Public Works personnel began laying and securing insulation over the site.

"My hope," Ronald said, "is that this will be very educational to our community; that it will bring us closer together as a community and as a people." The body was already a hot topic of discussion in the Barrow schools. An Iñupiat teacher at Ipalook Elementary School wanted her students to realize the man in the bluff was not just a body, not just a subject of curiosity, but a member of the community—a relative, a person to be treated with respect.

The teacher called him Uncle Foot. In an instant the name spread throughout the community. People liked it. By the time workers drove heavy spikes into the side of the giant blue tarp that had been stretched over the insulation, the man below had become everyone's Uncle Foot.

That night the Barrow City Council held an emergency meeting. With the advice and consent of the elders, who as keepers of traditional knowledge are highly respected and deferred to on matters of culture, the council agreed to an excavation the following summer and to an autopsy, stipulating that all aspects of both would be subject to the continued review and approval of the elders. Jack would oversee the actual excavation. The digging would be done largely by Iñupiat high school students. After the autopsy, Uncle Foot would be respectfully buried.

Night fell calm in Barrow. Down at the home of Uncle Foot, the National Guardsmen spent a

Right: A father and his tiny daughter retreat after viewing the stormy surf.

quiet night, and in the morning watched another day dawn clear, blue, warm, and still.

Jack arrived to inspect the protected site. After a good deal of removing, replacing, peering, and prodding, he expressed his satisfaction.

The ocean was calm. Looking seaward, the eye could see nothing but still water. Not one small piece of ice could be seen floating in the arctic sea. Reports coming in from aircraft and seismic vessels put the ice pack as far as two hundred miles offshore.

No one I spoke with could ever recall the pack having been so far away.

Many noted that this created prime conditions for an ivu of the type that might have killed Uncle Foot. With such a large stretch of open water, the wind and currents could well start the ice pack moving unimpeded toward Barrow. With no other ice to block its way, the pack could slam into the shoreline with the same force and power as it had some four hundred to five hundred years earlier, and with equal devastation. The modern homes and offices were no better equipped to withstand the force of tons of ice crashing in on them than were the iglus of old.

Freeze-up would be the salvation. Let everything freeze now, as it always did at this time of year. New, young ice would form on the sea and would act as a buffer against an advancing ivu.

That night another a meeting took place, this one between the regional tribal government—the Iñupiat Community of the Arctic Slope—and the Bureau of Indian Affairs (BIA). The two bodies had been engaged in a long-running dispute over the availability and use of tribal funds.

I entered the meeting hall and took a seat next to Ronald Brower. Outside, a stiff breeze had begun to blow. In the sea, whitecaps were rising.

The meeting began cordially. All expressed hopes that their differences could be resolved.

As the meeting wore on, the tribal representatives became ever more forceful in expressing what they wanted to do and how they wanted the BIA to assist. BIA representatives in their turn laid out guidelines they expected tribes to follow in order to receive BIA assistance.

As the debate grew, so too did the wind. It began to shriek around the corners of the building. The howl of the wind outside seemed to rise with the volume of the voices inside. I soon found myself paying far more attention to wind than to words. It blew harder, screaming and jolting the building. The voices rose even louder. Soon the building was shaking and rocking continuously, while raindrops pounded the walls, windows, and roof with a sound like that of thousands of tiny, stampeding hooves.

Suddenly, Earl Finkler appeared in the entry.

Without a word, Ronald leaped from his chair, grabbed his parka, and fled through the door, and I followed.

■ **Left:** Before the storms, a road ran across here and the surf broke farther back.

Down at the bluff, National Guardsmen held their position, but much farther back from the edge. Anyone venturing into the secured zone, now marked with only torn remnants of the yellow tape, risked his or her life. The wind had whipped the ocean into a roaring, black rage. Rain and sea spray mixed together indistinguishably, flying by in horizontal streaks that stung the face.

The hard wind forced us to lean into it just to keep standing. Gritty breakers churned the beach and slashed at the silt-and-ice bluff, cutting out its bottom and gushing over the top. The tarp had been ripped away, leaving only a tattered fragment that whipped the bluff top. The insulation had vanished. Had Uncle Foot gone with it?

With surf splashing over the bluff, no one was anxious to peer over its edge. Several of us formed a line with Dan Cox, the town's bottled-water distributor, at the head. We linked ourselves in a human chain and moved toward the edge, ready to jerk Dan back to safety should the bluff collapse beneath him. A breaker came roaring out of the darkness. We backpedaled as it boiled over the top. It receded. We rushed to the edge. Dan peeked over. Another breaker came surging in. Gushing surf again surged over the bluff, sending us reeling back.

"He's still here!" Dan shouted. "He's still here! We can save him!"

A few of us soon discovered that if we timed it right, we could slip briefly up to the edge a little off to the left side of Uncle Foot, catch a glimpse of him, and then scoot back. In the stormy, dim light of night, I could barely make out the gray outline of his leg, more exposed than earlier, just beneath the whipping tarp fragment.

Suddenly, as the sea receded just long enough to briefly expose a narrow strip of beach, a dark figure sprinted between the boiling surf and the eroding bluff. Whoever it was took a good look at Uncle Foot, then sprinted back to safe ground just ahead of the next surge of seawater.

I was surprised to see Ronald and Dan emerge through the black, driving rain and spray, struggling to drag a heavy, steel track rail.

Barrow is five hundred miles from the nearest railhead. Yet over the years, the commercial whalers, the Air Force, the Navy, and more recently the borough and the regional corporation have brought in by ship, barge, air, and Caterpillar train a bit of just about anything a person can think of.

"If we can place this across the tarp, so that it holds it over Uncle Foot, maybe we can save him," Ronald shouted.

I grabbed the rail. It was so cold my hands numbed before we could reach the bluff edge. We wedged the rail between the bluff edge and two thick driftwood poles that had framed the ancient iglu.

Right: Ronald H. Brower passes over Uncle Foot.

The rail lay across the top of the remaining tarp, but wind and spray still whipped the fragment in the air above Uncle Foot, giving him no protection at all.

Jonathan Aiken Sr. appeared with a truckload of four-by-eight-foot sheets of half-inch steel plates, each weighing several hundred pounds. It took at least two of us, and sometimes three, per side to carry the plates to the bluff edge.

We pushed the first one over the edge. It fell straight down, its weight driving it deep into the pebbly beach.

More plates were hauled to the edge and pitched over the side.

Soon a wall of steel plates stood between the surf and the bluff. Churning froth crashed into this steel wall and bounced harmlessly back toward the sea. We leaned into the wind, peered over the edge, and admired our handiwork.

"Well," Ronald shouted, "it looks like this might work!"

Out of the blackness, a giant wave suddenly loomed over us. We dashed back to safety as it exploded onto the beach and roared over the bluff top, flipping the steel plates about like playing cards in the hands of a drunken trickster.

Another great wave followed and ripped up the face of the bluff, hurling one end of the steel rail free and dropping it directly over Uncle Foot. The wave had inadvertently lodged the rail firmly between one of the old iglu poles and the bluff, where it held the tarp remnant directly over Uncle Foot. The crashing surf blasted into the tarp—but not into Uncle Foot.

Dan and Ronald drove a stake into secure ground and tied down the rail. Nothing more could be done.

I returned to the tiny room I rented in a narrow three-story house in town. I lay in bed, listening to the wind, feeling the house shake, thinking about how dramatic this had all been, this storm raging against Uncle Foot. Upon waking the next morning, I rushed back to the site.

The wind was stiff, but not so violent as the night before. Breakers twenty feet high thundered half a mile out at sea, churning the ocean into brown, silty froth.

Surf still charged up the beach to crash against the bluff, but between surges one could dash in, get a good look, and dash out. On each side of Uncle Foot's crushed home, the bluff had eroded severely, retreating several feet. But while being undercut, the permafrost holding Uncle Foot had held. His leg was now exposed nearly to the hip, but he was still frozen, still intact.

All along the waterfront, residents wandered through the wind, checking out the damage. The entire bluff area had eroded, putting houses and buildings at risk. The road crossing the spit between Barrow and its Browerville suburb had washed out. Power lines were down.

Left: Braving the thunderous surf, Harry Norton maneuvers a heavy metal drum into position, hoping to protect the bluff site holding Uncle Foot from further erosion.

Heavy-equipment operators from the Public Works department set out to repair the road and the downed lines and to throw up a levee to ward off future erosion along the beach and the spit. They secured three giant drums, each the size of a semitrailer, and filled them with sand and gravel.

As a crowd once again gathered atop the bluff to watch, Public Works employees Harry Norton and Thomas (Tom) Brower III drove two D-9 Caterpillars into the surf and began pushing and tugging at the drums. Waves crashed into the Cats and splashed over them, yet the men gradually maneuvered the filled drums, weighing between twenty and forty tons each, into place.

Several hours later, the drums finally formed a solid barricade between Uncle Foot and the surf. It was hoped that waves as fierce as those of the previous night would dissipate their energy on the drums and do no more harm to Uncle Foot.

Harry and Tom's effort had been heroic, witnessed by many.

The next day was calm. A small, gentle surf washed the beach. New insulation was placed over Uncle Foot. Another tarp was put in place and battened down even more securely than before.

Freeze-up would occur any day now. New ice would cover the ocean and protect the waterfront against an advancing ivu. Surf does not rise in a sea covered by ice. Uncle Foot would be protected. The autopsy and excavation next summer would take place.

One week after the big storm, the ocean was still ice free.

The weather was calm and beautiful and the silt from the storm had settled. The Chukchi was glassy and blue—not even a breeze ruffled its surface. Then a gentle gust, hardly noticeable, lightly rippled the water. But what started gently quickly grew strong and violent. As evening approached, giant waves were again building in the sea. I rushed to the bluff, where several people were already gathered. We were happy to see the drum blockade was doing its job and holding back the surf. We went home, to eat our dinners.

But it was as if the wind sensed that we had dismissed it, that we considered it beaten. It blew harder and harder, growing in fury until it topped sixty knots, then sixty-five, seventy, then seventy-five, eighty, then lashed the shore with hurricane force.

Again I fought my way to the bluff.

If it had been dark during the earlier storm, it was darker now. Walking against this wind was like climbing a steep hill. The effort left me breathless. In fear of being torn from my feet, I found myself grabbing for things—car door handles, the walls of pickup truck beds. To even approach the bluff edge was to ask for death. There was anger in the wind, anger in the sea.

I fought my way to within inches of Ronald. I could see that he was shouting at me, but could not make out his words.

"What?" I shouted back.

"There is nothing we can do," he answered. "Too dangerous."

As surf washed over the bluff, I found myself standing beside a young woman. She was shouting at me, but I could not make out her words.

"What?" I shouted back.

She shouted again.

"What?"

She dashed to the leeward side of a parked pickup. Her straight, black hair had been tossed by the wind and plastered down with water.

Right: National Guardsmen Perry Anashugak, James Itta, Lloyd Hopson, Bill Brown, John Ahyakak, and Vaughn Nungasak stand guard over the site.

"I haven't seen anything like this in twenty-eight years," she shouted. That was her age. "Do you think Uncle Foot is a shaman?"

"I don't know."

"Some people are saying he is a shaman. I didn't believe it. Now I think maybe he is."

"Maybe."

"I don't think he wants to be examined, picked apart."

"Maybe not."

Later, Glenn Roy Edwards would express the same suspicion. He told me he had been advised by his grandmother never to build a home on the land where Uncle Foot later appeared. There was a shaman in the ground there, she had warned, "buried face down with his head pointed toward hell."

In any case, the powers at work here had overpowered those of machines, human ingenuity, and intelligence. There was nothing to do now but go home and try to sleep.

Once I climbed into bed, the house shook so violently and the wind roared so loudly, I began to picture the whole structure toppling. I wondered what I would look like, being pulled from the rubble. Elsewhere, homes were being evacuated as surf beat at their doors. The foundations of structures standing on the bluff were being cut out from beneath them.

Sometime during that dangerous night, Uncle Foot left us.

No one saw him go, although Ronald thought maybe he had seen a foot rise out of the churning, black surf, then disappear. He couldn't be certain.

At daylight I returned to the beach. A new effort was being launched now to save the homes and buildings. George Leavitt's house stood on a higher part of the bluff overlooking the Chukchi. It now hung half over the sea. Surf slapped the beach some thirty feet directly beneath his living room. What had seemed solid ground was broken and split, revealing great slabs of ice beneath sod, exposing more ancient artifacts. The damage to Barrow was now in the millions of dollars.

By the next day, the wind had died. The sea began to calm.

I walked the beach in front of the remains of Uncle Foot's home. A wrinkled, pocked slab of maktak, perhaps centuries old, lay in the sand. Had Uncle Foot taken this whale? Snow began to fall. Cold stung my cheeks. The freeze was at last settling in.

The community gathered at city hall to talk about the storm and the visit of Uncle Foot, and to decide what to do if any more bodies in the many house mounds bordering the ocean were ever again uncovered. Some elders felt that, henceforth, all exposed bodies should be quickly recovered and buried. "Suppose the body found was a relative of mine," Gilford Mongoyak explained. "I would not wait until next year to bury it. I would do it now."

Left: During the final storm, no one saw Uncle Foot go, although Ronald Brower thought he might have seen a foot lift out of the black surf and disappear. He couldn't be certain.

Another elder, Patrick Okpeaha, who in his younger days had survived a days-long drift on a slab of ice, had words of solace. "A burial at sea is cleaner than any other burial," he said. "This is what happened to Uncle Foot."

Soon the tundra was blanketed in snow. Ice formed in the sea and quickly covered the rivers and lakes of the Arctic Slope.

The following summer, students from Barrow High School joined anthropologists to excavate what fragments were left of Uncle Foot's house. Among the artifacts was a shaman's amulet.

Right: Elder Patrick Okpeaha described a burial at sea as "the cleanest kind." Another elder, Thomas Brower Sr., walks along the beach as the stormy seas slowly quiet down.

"What the bow-
head whale is to
other communities,
that's what the
beluga is to us. We
succeed by working
together, everybody
in the village.
To us, the beluga
means food."

—AMOS AGNASSAGA

POINT LAY, population two hundred, sits 150
miles southwest down the coast from Barrow.
Each summer, near the Fourth of July, some three
thousand beluga whales—out of an Alaska population of forty-five thousand—migrate by, headed
northeast. In a hunt reminiscent of how the
Lakota of the Great Plains would cut out a
number of buffalo with their ponies from a much
larger herd, the hunters of Point Lay intercept
thirty to forty belugas and herd them into fifty-
mile-long Kasegaluk Lagoon.

There, in shallow water that prevents dead
whales from sinking out of sight, the hunters
harvest a year's worth of food in one day. They
also distribute belugas to other villages on the
Arctic Slope and in the Kobuk River basin to the
south. In turn, the hunters receive other foods
not taken locally, such as bowhead, large tasty
sheefish, and moose.

U.S. Fish and Wildlife Service marine biologist
Kathy Frost has extensively studied belugas and
observed the hunt. She praises the efficient manner of the hunt and supports the hunters' claim
that they pose no threat to the beluga population.
Other biologists agree, and the International
Whaling Commission has not yet sought to
assert authority over Native beluga hunts in
Alaska or Canada. The hunters of Point Lay have
joined others in forming the Alaska Beluga
Whale Committee, which has been cooperating
with biologists and discussing ways to ensure that
the hunt remains under Native management.

On a day when temperatures topped ninety, I
winged my way in the Running Dog, my single-
engine airplane, across the northern Interior,
through the Brooks Range, past Igloo Mountain,
and over the coastal plain to Point Lay, where a
heavy bank of fog shrouding the ocean raced me
to the runway. I landed just ahead of it.

■ **Previous page:** Biologists were on hand during the hunt to take specimens for biological study and toxicity samples. Edgar Anniskett talked biologist Geoff Carroll into giving him an eyeball. Then every kid wanted one.

■ **Left:** During a Fourth of July celebration in Point Lay, young Dorothy Henry won a "Big Sister" doll. She loved that doll and for many days afterward, everywhere Dorothy was seen, the doll was seen too.

Soon I walked through the heavy, cold fog as it drifted across the empty gravel streets of the village. A teenage girl emerged from the gray. "Hi," I said.

Saying nothing, she turned her face from mine, then disappeared hurriedly into the fog. I walked on. Two stalking figures materialized in silhouette out of the fog, atop a nearby rise. The front figure held a bow loaded with an arrow. He slipped quietly over the shrouded tundra a few steps in front of the other, then stopped. Both figures crouched. The boy in the lead raised the bow, drew back the arrow, and let it fly. Both boys chased after the arrow, disappearing into the fog once again.

I continued down to the water, where a dozen tiny aluminum skiffs quietly awaited the arrival of the belugas.

I studied the boats, then turned back toward the airport. Nesting birds of different species darted across the road in front of me, feigning injury, desperate to lure me away from nests I did not intend to bother. In front of me, slowly taking hazy shape like something from science fiction, the great white globe of the Distant Early Warning Line station appeared as a giant golf ball. The station, built to detect incoming Soviet, then Russian, missiles and aircraft, had brought great change to the people of Kali, or in Iñupiaq, the Kalimiut.

Traditionally, small groups of people had roamed this coast between Point Hope and Wainwright, camping wherever the animals were. One of the most popular locations was Kali, a mound of sod-covered frost that rises out of the sand spit separating Kasegaluk Lagoon from the Chukchi Sea. The people tell how an old woman living here went out to gather leaves to feed her grandson. Before departing, she admonished him not to look outside until her return. He grew restless and finally peeked outside. He spotted his grandmother dragging a piece of ground, rich with green leaves, back to their iglu. This disobedience prevented her from bringing the treat further. That piece of ground was transformed into the mound, Kali.

Kali provided good high and dry land. Many Kalimiut built houses there, as Kasegaluk Lagoon was a prime traditional site for harvesting belugas. In response to twentieth-century demands for schoolhouses and post offices, a permanent village formed and thrived.

Following construction and manning of the DEW Line station in the mid-1950s, life at Kali slipped into decline. "It was the alcohol," village Mayor Amos Agnassaga told me. "The DEW Line brought alcohol into the village. It really hurt the people." The military bar was open to a community that had never before had a convenient source of liquor. DEW Line personnel used drink as barter in the village.

Social problems grew. The quality of life

deteriorated. "The people who didn't drink left first," Amos recalled. "Then, after they closed the school in 1958, the whole village left."

Only Warren and Dorcas Neakok remained. They moved from the old village site on Kali across the lagoon into a hut near the Point Lay DEW Line station, where Warren went to work.

One summer, the Neakoks were off visiting relatives in Wainwright when DEW Line workers broke into their ice cellar. The vandals left the cellar open, exposing their entire food supply to summer temperatures. "Oh boy," Dorcas recalled in her biography, "everything was ruined. The ice cellar just filled up with water. There was nothing we could do."

Another time, the Neakoks noticed a helicopter buzzing back and forth from the DEW Line to old Kali. People were looting the fur clothing, skins, and other possessions of the Kalimiut. Dorcas rushed a message to the DEW Line: "Bring all the junks you pick from Old Village and bring them to me here. Right now!"

Left: Amos Agnassaga instructs Charlie Tuckfield to shoot in front of the belugas to turn them into Kasegaluk Lagoon.

Right: Beluga surfacing in Kasegaluk Lagoon.

They obeyed.

Once, the Neakoks left home for two weeks and returned to find an oil exploration well being drilled right in front of their door. No one had asked their permission or even considered paying them for the right. They just did it.

Still, there were good times for the Neakoks: the times their children returned for short visits.

"That's why we stayed here. I knew my children would come back," Dorcas recalled.

The people who left Kali took up residence from Barrow to the Lower 48.

Amos, for instance, ventured off to Chicago, where he became a diesel mechanic, and later to San Francisco. Amos enjoyed California. He found the weather nice, the people friendly. He played baseball and joined the California National Guard. Yet he longed for his hunting lifestyle. He fished with rod and reel, but it wasn't the same. In 1970 Amos took leave to bowhead hunt in Wainwright and never went back.

After passage of the Alaska Native Claims Settlement Act and formation of the North Slope Borough, the Kalimiut returned to reclaim their village, but moved it from Kali across Kasegaluk Lagoon to be near the DEW Line airport. This became the village of Point Lay.

⁓

By my third day in Point Lay, no belugas had been spotted. I flew Amos forty miles down the coast to an inlet at the south end of the lagoon.

Below us, thousands of belugas churned the Chukchi. From three thousand feet, they looked like little kernels of rice boiling to the surface. I flew high. A biologist once motored into the belugas and inadvertently scared them away. Villagers handed him a "blue ticket" out of Point Lay—a non-negotiable invitation to leave—and told him not to bother returning.

"You can go lower," Amos said. I dropped down to fifteen hundred feet, cut my power, and glided quietly down to eight hundred feet. The whales were spread through a five-mile stretch of ocean, most of them milling about within one mile of the beach. Some dug up silt from the bottom in search of food. Here and there, several whales crowded intently around a single beluga, which I reckoned must have been female. Some lolled lazily about; others rolled on their sides to look up at us. Belugas are among the tiniest of whales; adults average only about thirteen feet in length and weigh one and a half tons. Thanks to their comical bulbous heads and perpetually grinning expressions, these startling white whales are adored by school children worldwide. To the people of Point Lay, the belugas mean even more.

"I figured they would be here," Amos said. "It is good to know for sure. Sometimes they can hang around here for several days before moving on. We like to wait until they get closer to the village before we go and get them."

Left: Robert Long and Bob Tuckfield, hunting beluga in Kasegaluk Lagoon.

After we returned, Amos introduced me to his friend Charlie Tuckfield, a short, good-humored, middle-aged man. Charlie agreed to take me with his crew during the hunt.

The next day was the Fourth of July. That morning marine biologist Kathy Frost returned from a research flight and announced that the whales were beginning to move toward the village. Amos said, "If they're starting to move today, it will take them about two days to get here. Today we got the Fourth of July to celebrate."

So we celebrated under a hot sun, eating hot dogs, hamburgers, and bowhead maktak, and competed in Eskimo baseball, other games, and races of many kinds—all the while being dined on by hordes of mosquitoes.

The next morning I walked to the tiny village store, which had but a small selection of very expensive food. A woman stood over the modestly stocked meat freezer, gazing with dismay at frozen beef and chicken.

"Yeeuck," she said. "I'm tired of this kind of stuff. It's making me sick. I can't wait for the belugas!"

Days passed. Finally the belugas began to move in earnest, but gale winds churned the sea into frothing white. We waited for the wind to die, but it only grew stronger, raging throughout the next day and periodically blowing in heavy layers of fog. It blew into the following day as well, then finally began to diminish; we would wait one more day for the sea to calm.

While we waited, I took Amos for an early morning flight. Silently he gazed out the Running Dog's window over a sea seemingly emptied of belugas.

Upon returning to Point Lay, he went off to ponder the situation and to solicit advice from the other hunters. Kathy also came in from a beluga survey flight. She had spotted just one pod of about thirty, some twenty miles out from Five Mile Inlet. Amos heard this news with a long face.

Resigned to what seemed an interminable wait for something that might not ever happen, I sat down to read a copy of the *Anchorage Daily News*. Charlie Tuckfield strolled in, wearing rubber boots.

"Are you coming?" he asked.

Half an hour later we were in the water— Charlie, his son Bob, Robert Long, and myself. Charlie steered from the stern, Bob sat by him, Robert and I occupied the middle.

We skimmed across the lagoon toward the inlet. Kicking up white water on both sides of us were the other members of the fourteen-boat flotilla. I could see Amos guiding one of them.

"We've got sandwiches," Bob said, motioning toward the ice chest. "Spam and ham. Help yourself. Pop, too. Pepsi, root beer, 7-Up. I don't know if you eat *ugruk*. We got ugruk too." I reached into the icebox and found the dried meat of the bearded seal. The braided muscle tissue was thick and black. Though hard on the outside,

Right: Once the first shot is fired, the hunt proceeds to its end very quickly.

the slightly moist insides gave it a chewy texture. Washed down with Pepsi, it was exquisite. "You like ugruk?" Charlie asked, surprised. Saying nothing, I just smiled and took another piece.

We passed through the inlet, into the Chukchi Sea. It was sunny and warm. The green water rolled in gentle waves, with hardly a breeze to ripple the surface. All boats turned south, then fanned out into one long line, perpendicular to the shore, to comb the ocean.

Bob and Robert stood frequently to gaze out over the water or to glass it with binoculars. Charlie did the same.

We traveled slowly, at about five knots, and after thirty minutes a boat to the seaward side of us suddenly gunned forward. We did the same, as did other nearby boats. Spray flew into the skiff as we bounced over the waves. Just as suddenly, power was cut in the boat that had begun this dash and it returned to a slow pace. The other boats did likewise. Whatever had been seen, it was not beluga. This process repeated itself several times until Robert finally shouted, "I see white whales!" He handed the binoculars to Bob.

"Yes," Bob confirmed. "White whales! I see them too."

Charlie took the glasses. "I see something white, all right. I'm not sure what." He returned to his duties as driver. Robert and Bob kept scanning. I could see little arcs of white in the distance, appearing and disappearing, the way

belugas do when they roll through the sea.

"It's beluga, all right." Robert said.

"It's beluga!" Bob agreed.

"Well, let's go have a look." Charlie sounded unconvinced.

He gunned the engine, and the nose of the boat lifted out of the water. We ricocheted across the waves, throwing spray behind us. On both sides of us, other boats did likewise.

We closed to within half a mile of the white arcs. Charlie cut the power. The nose of the boat dropped.

"Just waves, breaking on the beach," Charlie said.

We all turned seaward once again.

For hours we motored along under a pleasant sun, chewed dry ugruk, drank Pepsi, made short, fast, furious runs, and in the end saw no belugas.

Finally Amos sent out the signal to return to the inlet for a meeting.

Charlie applied the throttle. Soon we pulled into a narrow width of water, wedged between two sand spits jutting slightly past each other. Hands reached out to grab us as we pulled alongside a boat to create a raft. We did the same to the next boat, captained by Jack Long and crewed by Nick Hank, Jack's longtime girlfriend, Bertha, and their five-year-old son Sluggo, who wielded a BB gun. Sluggo, by far the youngest person on the hunt, had won the boat in a Fourth of July lottery in Barrow. He agreed to let his parents use it if they took him along.

Left: Once the whales are landed, women and children come by the boatload to help with the butchering and distribution.

Amos stood up. "Where are the belugas?" he asked. "Maybe they went north." If the hunters did not find them soon, this year would pass with no belugas harvested in Point Lay. It would be a great hardship for all.

"Maybe they didn't go north," someone said. "Maybe they got spooked by something." It could have been a boat, a low-flying plane, a killer whale. "Maybe they're scattered at sea."

"Maybe we should try going north," Amos suggested. Everyone agreed. It was 5:00 P.M. "Everybody go home for one hour. Get something to eat. We'll meet back here at 6:00 P.M. Then we'll go north."

One hour—plenty of time for me to take a little flight in that direction.

"I'll go with you," Robert said.

Flying half a mile offshore, we traveled north to Ten Mile Inlet, then fifteen miles beyond. No belugas. I turned back. We reached Point Lay, then continued on south. In the distance, in rippled water backlit to create a shimmering effect, I could see one dull-looking triangular patch of water, which had the appearance of a small oil slick. I edged my way toward it. Elongated shapes gradually began to take shape in the triangle.

Belugas.

Each whale was pointed in the same direction, northwest, moving steadily seaward at about a twenty-degree angle from the shoreline. There were at least twenty, maybe thirty. They were

about ten miles offshore.

We returned and reported our finding to Amos. He called the hunters together for another meeting. They abandoned the idea of going north and agreed to go south.

Soon we were in the water again.

Hours passed. We found nothing.

"Let's go home, boys" Charlie said. "Get some sleep. Maybe we can find the belugas another day." As we tied down the boat, he laughed and joked but could not hide the pain in his eyes, the frustration in his smile. It was about 10:00 P.M The sun shone warm and bright. Bob noted that a few of the boats had not returned.

"They'll probably be back soon," Robert said.

Half an hour passed. I grew restless and took a walk. The sun hung low over the northern horizon, casting a golden glow on the village. I heard a roar, coupled with female laughter. Six young girls who were piled on the same four-wheeler rocketed by me, kicking up dust and little stones.

An out-of-work sled dog, chained to a stake by the corner of a house, barked viciously, then wagged its tail weakly and whined as I spoke back to it.

A group of young men lounged about the yard and on the roof of an old shack in the process of being renovated. One had a new motorcycle, which he showed to me with great pride. He wore a black leather jacket with matching boots. His jet-black hair hung well past his shoulders. He would have looked at home among bikers I have known in California.

Robert sat among those on the roof.

"Don't worry," he assured me, "if something comes up, we'll get you out of bed. Go get some sleep."

⌒

Half an hour later, I was out walking again, and half an hour after that.

By 1:30 A.M. I could take it no longer. "I'm going to fly down the coast, see if I can spot a boat," I announced.

Robert jumped down from the roof. "Mind if I come?"

We flew past the end of Kasegaluk Lagoon and saw nothing. We pushed on for another ten miles. I grew worried that if I did not turn around immediately, my nearly empty tanks would run dry before we could reach Point Lay.

"Maybe they went north," Robert speculated as I went into my U-turn. The low northerly sun reflected in a glitter off ripples on the water ahead of us.

Right: Five-year-old Sluggo Henry agreed to let his parents, Jack Henry and Bertha Tazruk, use the boat he won in a Barrow lottery, but only if they brought him along on the hunt.

I had been flying about half a mile out and banked the Dog toward shore.

"Beluga!" Robert shouted. Directly below us, a small number of white backs appeared in the water, a short distance from the beach.

"Boats," I added.

I cut my power and finished the turn in a glide. The hunters had formed an open box around a pod of belugas. The shoreline served as one side of the box. Two boats running in a perpendicular line from the shore made up the back. Three remaining boats, widely separated, traveling parallel to the shore, formed the seaward edge. The box was open to the north. The whales swam toward the opening, which continually moved away from them. Individual whales broke the surface just long enough to catch their breath, then disappeared. Still, we could tell there were at least twenty, maybe thirty.

I put on the power and beelined back to Point Lay.

Half an hour after touchdown, I again sat in Charlie's boat as it slashed the sea. This time we knew belugas were ahead of us. We traveled fast.

Over the water, layers of stratus clouds drifted through a pastel sky in which a pale moon hung. Toward the mountains, cumulus clouds, formed in the heat of the previous day, still towered. The low Arctic sun was moving over the northern horizon toward the east. Eider ducks, geese, and murres flapped by in determined little groups.

Sometimes we would find them resting on the water. In a panic they would slap the sea with their wings and their running webbed feet until lift overcame gravity and they became airborne. Kittiwakes passed over us, peering inside the boat.

After a couple of hours, the other boats appeared in the distance. Charlie diminished the power. Sitting in the lead boat, Amos signaled for us to fall in behind him. We did, and settled in at a very slow pace.

"You see them?" Charlie asked. "You see the belugas?"

"I see them," Bob said.

The belugas, at least a third of a mile away, traveled near the shoreline. Keeping low profiles, they barely broke the surface upon sounding. Yet they could not hide the vapor of their breath. Suddenly a small group charged past the boats and into the open sea. Two boats roared to life and set off after them, cutting through the water in sharp turns. When the boats returned, I could not tell if they brought the escapees with them.

Traveling no faster than two or three knots, we watched in silence as blasts of belugas' breath caught the light of the sun.

Bob finally broke the silence. "They're doomed," he said.

There was nothing to do now but settle in for the long ride back to the village, and to suffer the cold. Despite the earlier heat, the twenty-four-hour sun, and the beautiful night, the chill

■ **Left:** "The belugas are smarter than we are," a hunter told me. "If we fight and quibble over them, if we don't use them wisely and respect their gift, they will know, and they will go somewhere else."

Left: Biologists who have studied the one-day hunt give the people of Point Lay high marks for the efficient manner in which they carry it out. For centuries, the beluga have continued to return to the people of Point Lay.

sank through my Levi's and my thermal underwear. It penetrated my rubber boots, two pairs of heavy wool socks, and brought pain to my feet and toes. It seeped in through my heavy jacket, the lighter one beneath, and the sweater and wool shirts underneath it. What foolishness had overcome me, to cause me to be here without my arctic gear?

Just offshore from Five Mile Inlet, where the hunters planned to turn the belugas into Kasegaluk Lagoon, I noticed Amos standing in his now still boat, frantically waving to us. Charlie interpreted this as a signal for us to hold steady. He cut power. This caused Amos to wave more frantically. Charlie throttled up and raced to Amos's boat. Amos shouted for Robert to trade places with him. Amos then jumped into our boat, and Robert into Amos's.

"We're out of gas!" Amos shouted over our engine. "Those belugas are going to escape." He waved at the whales, who were beginning to charge past the mouth of the inlet in what would soon be a dash for the open sea.

"We've got to turn them back. Get out your rifle!"

Amos took over the driving as Charlie shoved a clip into his rifle. Amos raced the engine, maneuvering in sharp turns to place us in position between the belugas and the open sea. Somehow, Bob, Charlie's son, slept through all this.

In seconds Amos had the boat where he wanted it.

"Shoot!" he shouted.

From a position alongside his sleeping son, Charlie took aim, then fired. The bullet kicked up spray close to the lead belugas. Bob jerked awake.

"Shoot more in front!" Amos barked. "If the lead ones get past, the rest will follow." Bob pulled out his own rifle. Father and son began firing round after round into the water between the belugas and the open sea. The belugas pulled up short.

Soon the remainder of the flotilla had formed an arch between the belugas and the open sea, facing the inlet. Amos returned to his refueled boat, and Robert returned to ours.

Slowly the boats advanced on the belugas. Hunters pounded the front of their boats with boots, rifle butts, and bare hands. A sound not unlike that of an enthusiastic football crowd pounding their feet on aluminum bleachers rose over the water. As this gauntlet drew down upon the belugas, the whales gathered together in mass, holding their position.

Then one beluga slipped through the inlet, into the lagoon. The rest quickly followed.

The hunters pursued, then formed a line behind the whales, pushing them toward the shallow water in front of Kali.

At the pace we were traveling, our final destination was still at least two hours away. I could feel the tingle of warmth returning to my legs and feet. The sun was rising higher. Cold discomfort was over for this day. Riding alongside us was Sluggo's boat with the young boy himself perched proudly in the bow, clutching his BB gun, seriously scanning the water ahead.

Suddenly a beluga dashed between our boats, traveling in the opposite direction. Jack Long broke formation, easily outran the whale, and turned it back. Up in the distance, I could see the cemetery on Kali. A large white, snowy owl perched atop a white cross. Lying on the beach below was the giant bleached jawbone of a bowhead whale, caught decades earlier by a Wainwright crew and brought here, where it will ultimately stand over a hunter's grave.

The hunters allowed considerable distance to grow between the boats and the whales. Occasionally a beluga would rise up vertically from the water and look back at us.

As we neared the shallow water in front of Kali, the distance began to close. Whales began to dart about at close range, splashing powerfully. The water grew choppy as the wake of boats and belugas collided.

Caught between the boats and the rush of belugas, eighteen eider ducklings fought panic as three female ducks ushered them toward safety. As motorboats and white whales passed close by on all sides, two of the adult ducks lost their nerve. Squawking in protest, they flapped away, leaving one mother to doggedly guide the youngsters through the commotion.

Left: A small boy sees the belugas as a good place to play. Ann Tukrook tells him otherwise.

Bob and Robert slipped loaded clips into their rifles. "Shoot when we are right by the whale," Charlie instructed. "Never shoot when there is another boat in front of you. Be careful. You don't want to shoot your partner."

Bob and Robert took standing positions toward the front of the boat. On both benches, boxes of ammunition stood ready.

The roar of an outboard engine gunning to full throttle rose suddenly.

"It's starting!" Bob shouted. About fifty yards in front of us, a boat in silhouette rushed through the choppy water. A figure standing in the bow pointed a rifle into the water, then jerked back with the kick. In front of the boat the water churned with the thrashing of white flukes. The gunner quickly followed with a second shot. The thrashing stopped.

Instantly we were in the thick of it.

Whales charged in every direction, whipping their flukes in confusion, churning up silt from the bottom. Belugas bumped each other and did not know which way to go. On all sides of us, boats pulled alongside belugas. Blasts shattered the air. Bullets pierced flesh, and blood dyed the water red.

Charlie steered to the side of a whale. Bob opened fire. I was too close to his barrel, and the percussive shock wave slammed into my left ear with stabbing pain. The animal rolled over, dead. Water and blood rained down upon us. From

starboard, a beluga charged blindly at the boat. Grabbing both gunwales, I braced myself. The whale slammed headlong into the boat, rocking it violently. The animal slid beneath us, then emerged on the other side. Bob shot it dead. Gunners in other boats in every direction did the same. For a brief moment, I considered the possibility that a bullet fired from another boat could ricochet off the water and rip me right out of the boat into the water, where my blood would mingle with that of the belugas.

In what felt to be no more than minutes, all the belugas herded into the shallow area had been shot. Most lay belly-up in the water. A few still had life in them.

"Let's get the wounded," Charlie commanded. As did the hunters in the other boats, we tracked down belugas that were still moving, however weakly, and ended their suffering. Robert spotted a slightly wounded beluga. It swam quietly, keeping its profile low, past two freshly killed whales. Charlie guided the boat. Bob fired. Simultaneously, the beluga lifted both head and flukes out of the water, arching its body in a graceful curve. It looked straight at us, then died. I was not unmoved by the death of this beluga, or of the others. My heart felt each bullet; I felt the life as it left these beautiful, graceful creatures, and it was a humbling thing to feel.

The hunters felt it as well. All action in the boat stopped. All voices fell silent.

Right: As mosquitoes swarm in incomprehensible numbers, Nick Hank taunts the batter just before lobbing his pitch during a Fourth of July game of "Eskimo Baseball."

Left: Nick Hank holding a beluga's tail, which is highly valued for both flavor and nutrition.

Charlie guided the boat alongside a floating carcass. Bob gaffed the animal, then with Charlie directing, he and Robert tied it to the boat and hauled it to shore. Soon all but a few belugas had been brought in. They now lay, tail first, on the beach, just below the cemetery.

Feeling exhausted from well over twenty-four hours with no sleep, I climbed half way up the mound of Kali, then plopped myself down in the grass. Nick Hank came and sat alongside me.

It was as fine a summer day as one could hope to find, anywhere.

A few hunters had returned to the village to catch a couple hours of sleep. Others lay on the beach, dozing. A boat full of women and children was making its way over from the village side of the lagoon. Others had already arrived. More would soon follow.

A tiny boy played along the edge of the water, picking up sticks, pebbles, and weathered beluga bones. He tossed these into the water between the whale carcasses.

The last boat brought the last whale to shore. A hunter wearing rubber boots jumped out of the boat and into the water as another on the shore came out to greet him. Together they unlashed the beluga from the boat and dragged it tail-first as far shoreward as possible. They then found themselves a comfortable place on the shore and dropped down to rest.

Sitting still and quiet, I absorbed the rays of the sun, grateful for their warmth. In front of me, the water was blue and glass-calm. Scattered along the beach, stretched-out hunters slept under the sun. Flippers and flukes reflected in the placid water took on the shapes of graceful white butterflies, stilled in flight. Gathering seagulls hung quietly in the sky.

In time, a group of men and women gathering on the beach began shouting for all to join them. They were ready to haul the belugas out of the water.

A line was attached to the flukes of the first whale. "All hands!" Someone shouted. "All hands!" Others joined the chorus. All grabbed the rope. "Walk away!" came the next command. In unison with the hunters, I threw my full weight into the task. Grunting and shouting, we trudged up the beach until the whale slid out of the water. We repeated the process several times.

The lines were dropped. All attention shifted to the butchering. Men and women wielding rounded *ulu* knives and long-handled, homemade knives cut rectangular incisions through the skin and blubber. As they cut, other workers hooked an edge or corner of the rectangle with *niksiks*—grappling hooks attached either to ropes or poles. These hookers pulled hard as the cutters diverted their attention to the underside of the rectangular slabs. Gradually the maktak was peeled from the body, making a breaking, crackling noise as it went.

A hooker would spike a slab of maktak at a good balance point, then carry it a short distance up Kali to drop in a large pile. Or a cutter would slash a handhold into the top of a couple of the slabs, and another person would lug them, one in each hand, off to the same pile. The slabs were warm to the touch, slick with oil, and heavy—about twenty-five to fifty pounds each.

Once the maktak was removed, the dark red meat below was cut into long lengths and carried to the piles. Flukes and flippers were cut off whole, then taken to the same place.

Soon it seemed like all there were but one family. People laughed, joked, and smiled. Tiny children ran about, playing games, laughing and squealing.

Finally all the beluga whales were transformed into several large piles of maktak and meat.

Happily tired, the villagers gathered together just below Kali, where coffee brewed on Coleman stoves and beluga maktak boiled in large pots.

"We have had a successful hunt," Amos pronounced. "It is time to give thanks for it."

Amos yielded to the elder Warren Neakok. "Thank you, Lord, for this food you have given to our village," Warren prayed. "We thank you for such a beautiful land, and for the life-giving sea. We thank you for the belugas, Lord. We ask you to bless the belugas, those that have given themselves today so that we can live, and those that still swim in the sea."

Right: Bertha Tazruk at work. All Point Lay families will get a generous share of the meat. Some people have come from other villages to help, and they too will get a share. Portions will also go to college students, loved ones in uniform, and others living away from home.

Then we ate maktak, boiled and topped with mustard. There were hot Eskimo donuts, coffee, and tea. It was delicious.

After the feast, the big piles were divided into smaller piles, one for each family of the community and for families from other villages who had sent people to help. A large pile was set aside for Iñupiat elders residing at the Senior Center in Barrow. The flesh of these belugas would work its way into every village on the North Slope, to others in the Kobuk River basin, and to loved ones in Anchorage, Fairbanks, and points Outside.

Small children joined adults in hauling pieces to the different share piles. Despite the long hours and the hard work, not a sad face could be seen. The smiles, the laughter continued. There was no grumbling, no complaining. Just people working together, using modern techniques but from within an ancient tradition, to feed their families with the food provided by their ancestral home.

I returned to Point Lay in November, when it was minus forty-six at midday as the village prepared for Thanksgiving. Belugas would be the central focus of the feast, but there would be many other foods, like caribou and ducks. A good supply of bowhead maktak and meat had come down from Wainwright. From the Kobuk River villages came sheefish. Turkey was shipped in by the North Slope Borough. I found that eating the Native food felt better than eating the turkey. It gave me more courage to face the cold.

The morning after the feast, I walked down a Point Lay street. A hard wind picked the snow from the ground and hurled it through the air, dimming the light of a low sun that, after this day, would not rise above the horizon again until mid-January. A young woman walking alone down the road nodded a shy "Hi" as she passed in the opposite direction. In front of me, a young man stepped into the street. A big smile spread across his face as he recognized the woman. He gave me a warm hello, then ran to catch her. He took her hand, and the two of them disappeared into the blowing snow. The young man was Carl Stalker, who, I had discovered during nighttime visits to the gym, loved basketball. He also loved the woman, Rhoda Long, who carried their child.

Just weeks later, the same couple encountered a polar bear a short distance from where I had seen them. Armed only with a pocketknife, Carl stepped between Rhoda and the bear so that she and their unborn child might live. He died fighting it off.

Right: As the noon sun barely manages to skim the southern horizon before disappearing for two months, Carl Stalker and Rhoda Long walk together in Point Lay. Carl was killed by a polar bear shortly after this photograph was taken. (An optical illusion causes the distant horizon to appear elevated over the local surroundings.)

IN THE FALL OF 1988, Roy Ahmaogak's father put Roy in charge of his whaling crew. Ralph Ahkivgak, better known as Malik, agreed to be Roy's harpooner. Malik, a short, slight man in his sixties, was highly respected for his exceptional skill as a harpooner and for his knowledge of animals and the environment. "In the distance, we will see a whale go down," Roy said. "'Turn that way, to the right,' Malik says. 'Go there.' We do, and there the whale is. Malik knows."

"Malik" means "follow." When Malik was a small boy, he had eagerly followed his father out to the whale hunt. He grew to become a great hunter, but never a captain. Few surpassed Malik in his knowledge of the sea, the ice, the land,

and the animals, yet he could never quite adjust to modern life. In town this bachelor lived on the fringe, never stockpiling the resources a captain must have to outfit a crew. If this bothered him, he did not show it. He seemed happy to contribute his skills to the success of whatever crew he traveled with. His bowhead kills were said to number in the scores, yet in his weathered face was a gentle softness, a quick and easy smile.

On October 7, Roy drove his snowmachine to Plover Point, where the sand spit reaching up to form Point Barrow bends a short distance to the southeast and ends. The year's bowhead allotment for Barrow had been met, and Roy's crew, with Malik's harpoon, had landed the last whale just over two weeks earlier. Heavy ice to the east, however, had prevented the whalers of Nuiqsut from going out, and should their quota allocation be passed on to Barrow, Roy wanted to be ready to go again. From Plover Point he could see that ice conditions were unusually heavy for the season. About five miles offshore, big pressure ridges had already piled up, and between these and the beach, slush covered the water.

Roy was startled to suddenly see three

California gray whales surfacing in the slush. Staying together, the three swam all about the immediate area, opening holes in the slush to breathe. They seemed confused. Having spent their summer feeding in the Arctic, the gray whales should have been well on their way to their mating grounds in Baja, California.

Roy rushed back to Barrow to tell his dad, his uncle George Ahmaogak, and Malik of his find. They returned to the site and watched as the whales continued struggling to take breath in the gathering ice.

George, who was also the mayor, felt compassion for these whales, which were not the whales he hunted. He called the North Slope Borough wildlife management office in Barrow and left word for biologists Geoff Carroll and Craig George, asking if anything could be done to help the trapped gray whales return to the open sea.

On October 12, Geoff and Craig took Oren Caudle from the North Slope Borough TV studio out to videotape the whales, still struggling in the slush between the shore and the ice pack. The biologists wanted to study the tape, then decide the best course of action. I headed out shortly afterward, following hunter Billy Adams, who worked for the wildlife management office and was assisting the biologists. So far, thin ice had prevented anyone from approaching the whales.

About one hundred yards from where we parked our snowmachines, I saw a dark hole in the slush, less than twenty feet in diameter. A hundred yards beyond was an almost identical hole. A frozen seagull lay belly down at the ice edge. We stood silently for five minutes.

Suddenly a bullet-shaped, barnacle-encrusted snout, cut by a grim, ever-frowning mouth, lunged out of the near hole, rose about four feet over the ice, and let loose a blast of spray that fanned out into the cold. Two smaller whales followed in rapid succession. All three settled down to bob and breathe as the bulk of their huge bodies extended, unseen, down at an angle under the slush surrounding the hole.

After about four minutes, the whales submerged and disappeared. Six minutes later, they reappeared in the more distant hole, where they went through the same cycle.

"They say gray whales are mean when you harpoon them," Billy said, explaining why the Iñupiat do not normally hunt them. "The maktak's not very good—thin, filled with barnacles. The steaks are supposed to be real good—if they're not stressed too bad. These whales are pretty stressed."

Overnight the slush hardened sufficiently to walk on. I flew back to the site with borough search-and-rescue helicopter pilot and hunter Price Brower and whaling captain Ben Itta.

We crept to the edge of the nearest hole. Suddenly the largest whale burst out with a great blast, raining spray down upon us. Soon all three

Previous page: Three gray whales, trapped in a hole in young ice off Plover Point.

Right: For days after their discovery, dangerous ice conditions kept humans away from the whales. When the ice began to thicken, the first person to venture out to the holes was helicopter pilot and whale hunter Price Brower.

whales had settled down for four minutes of bobbing and breathing. Price dropped to his hands and knees, edged up to the hole, reached out, and touched a whale. It jerked backward. Price did it again. Again the whale jerked back, but not as quickly or as far.

The first contact between a human being and these whales had been made, and that human was a whale hunter.

By this time, Oren's taped footage had made its way to Anchorage's Channel 2 news and,

through the NBC affiliate network, had been broadcast to the world. The world's attention was suddenly riveted on these three whales, facing what would have been a natural death were it not being broadcast on TV.

—

Early the next morning, NBC interviewed Geoff and Craig on the beach in front of Barrow's Top of the World Hotel. Media and government brass were pouring into town. Chief among them was red-haired Ron Morris of the National

Left: Price Brower reaches out and makes the first physical contact between the whales and humans.

Oceanic and Atmospheric Administration (NOAA), who chatted with the two biologists and their boss, Tom Albert, after the interview.

"When an animal's in trouble, you want to help it," Craig said. "You help it either by getting it over its trouble or, if you can't do that, you kill it and put it out of its misery." Geoff said the Barrow Whaling Captains were meeting that night to decide what to do about the gray whales.

"Wait a minute," Morris said, his intent green eyes flashing. "I must remind you that under the Marine Mammal Protection Act, all jurisdiction and any decision is up to the federal government."

I snowmachined to the site, arriving that morning before anyone else. For one treasured hour, I had the whales to myself. Looking down from the edge of one of the holes, the water appeared clear, deep green, almost black under the ice. Following a period of waiting, a huge dark form appeared, rising swiftly from the depths, its bulk magnified by the water. Muted shades of gray and green, speckled with all the hues of the rainbow, glimmered in flesh covered by barnacles and marred by red gashes. These colors grew quickly in intensity as the mass rose. The surface of the water rose just a little bit before breaking as the whale erupted out of the sea, shooting off a big blast of spray with a loud, hollow-sounding whoosh. Its two companions quickly followed, then all three whales settled down to bob and breathe. Their blowholes

flared open and closed as the air rushed in and out of their lungs. Gray whales can grow to nearly fifty feet in length and weigh up to forty tons. Biologists estimated these three juveniles to range between twenty-five and thirty feet.

The bottom jaw of the largest whale was somewhat out of alignment with the top jaw. The blowhole of the second whale was ornamented with a bonnet of barnacles. The flesh on the snout of the smallest whale had been so badly scraped that bone was exposed. It breathed with a terrible wheeze. The whales would soon be given names: Crossbeak, Bonnet, and Bone. In Iñupiaq they became Siku, Poutu, and Kannick.

In time, I heard the distant whine of snowmachines, followed by the drone of a helicopter. Soon I was no longer alone, now joined by the biologists, Ron Morris, Arnold Brower Jr., Arnold's wife and children, and others.

Despite some early misgivings, Arnold had come to study the situation, planning to report back to that night's meeting of the Barrow Whaling Captains. Carrying a long walking stick, Arnold stepped to the edge of a breathing hole. He saw that it was a small place. Slush floated within, hardening into ice near the edges. Arnold turned to walk away. A whale surfaced with the usual blast. The whale hunter turned quickly back to look at it. The other whales followed, settling in to bob and breathe. Four minutes later, Arnold saw them retreat—not by rolling their backs as they normally would, but by pulling their snouts awkwardly down through the ice.

"They would be more comfortable if the holes were bigger," Arnold said. Using small chain saws, biologists and hunters began cutting blocks from the edge of the ice to create a larger opening for the whales. More hunters, including Johnny Aiken, soon arrived and pitched in. After cutting a block, someone would grab it with a hook and pull the edge up over the lip of the hole. A rope would be attached. "*Kiita!*" someone would holler, the Iñupiaq command for "Let's go!" "All hands! Walk away!" Just like landing a bowhead, the whalers would grunt and shout, then pull the chunk of ice out of the water and away from the hole.

In the evening the Barrow Whaling Captains gathered outside the borough assembly room. Opinions were mixed on whether there should be a humane killing or a rescue effort. Before the meeting, Malik had quietly expressed his view that the whales should be killed, their torture ended. An NBC TV crew was waiting in the hallway. Arnold Brower Sr. called the hunters in and brought the meeting to order. Some of the hunters wanted to keep NBC out in the hall. Arnold Sr. had been a leader in the political and economic battle the Iñupiat waged to save their homeland and way of life. He understood the force of public opinion and the wrath of media

snubbed. He invited NBC in.

Arnold Sr. did not mention the possibility of killing the gray whales. He turned the discussion to the habits of different whale species, noting how belugas would follow bowheads out of danger, but grays would not. He speculated on what might happen if the whalers were to cut a path to open water for the whales. Would the grays follow? Would they save themselves or just get into trouble all over again? The hunters could at least give them a chance.

To the east, the Prudhoe Bay oil industry had also taken an interest in the gray whales. VECO, the major provider of oil-field services at Prudhoe Bay, volunteered to send a giant hoverbarge to break open a path for the whales. Towed by a Sikorski Skycrane—a giant elongated helicopter designed to hoist huge loads—the hoverbarge rides on a cushion of forced air, breaking the ice beneath it apart. The National Guard had agreed to provide a Skycrane. The whalers decided they would keep the whales' air holes in the ice open long enough to give the hoverbarge time to clear a path.

Morris agreed to the plan, but set a deadline: Tuesday, three days hence. He did not say what steps he would take should that deadline not be met.

The next day dawned cold and grew colder, settling in at minus seventeen degrees Fahrenheit. "You wouldn't believe the conversations I have

■ **Right:** Arnold Brower Jr. came out to inspect the situation on behalf of the Barrow Whaling Captains. Based largely on his report, the captains would decide whether to give the whales a quick and humane death or launch a rescue effort.

had with my superiors in Washington, D.C.," Morris told several of us sharing a car ride to the search-and-rescue hangar. "The president wants these whales saved. Whatever it takes, he wants them out of the ice holes and set free. Ronald Reagan wants to go out of office as an environmentalist." Contacts had been made with Soviet officials to see if they might send an ice-breaker, now operating some 350 miles to the north, Morris said, stressing that the information was confidential. Out at the holes, we were joined by the NBC camera crew.

The hoverbarge had encountered problems and was making little progress in the journey from Prudhoe Bay. Meanwhile, a crew of hunters had been hired by the borough to keep the air holes open, under Arnold Brower Jr.'s oversight. Malik was brought on and took the role of the knowledgeable elder hunter. Arnold's crew boss, Johnny Leavitt, did not want to wait for the hoverbarge. He wanted to begin cutting holes seaward. "We can do it," he grumbled to me. "That thing is never going to make it here."

Shortly after, I saw whaling captain James Matumeak observing the whales as they pushed their lacerated snouts through the abrasive, freez-ing slush. "Poor people," he said with a grimace.

By Tuesday the hoverbarge had made no progress. President Reagan called Prudhoe Bay to commend rescuers for their efforts. He urged them on.

The media had invaded in force: All the major American networks, Fuji Japan, Good Morning Britain, Australian TV, *People* magazine, *The London Mail*, and scores more, with more still coming. Barrow's four hotels overflowed. For tidy little profits, residents hosted journalists in their homes. Greenpeace arrived. The National Guard was everywhere.

———

Everyone involved was now trapped, forced to continue on, to seek solution after failed solu-tion, regardless of cost, time, and risk to human life. Helicopters beat the air continually, with as many as a dozen people in a single chopper. Journalists who could not find space in helicop-ters hired hunters to tow them on sleds, and paid astounding amounts of money for a fifteen-mile ride. Climbing the steps of the Top of the World Hotel, I was met by a wide-eyed Johnny Aiken coming down, counting a wad of buried hundred-dollar bills shoved into his hands by a TV crew he had hauled to the site. Journalists were dumped into the Arctic wearing inadequate ski clothing. And when those clothes were red, the journalists had to face an angry Arnold Brower Jr., for he knew whales were frightened by red. Meanwhile, the oil industry had put its Arctic expertise and credibility on the line and now had to come up with a solution that worked.

Yet in the midst of all this hoopla, something real was happening. In the faces of all these

Left: After images of the three whales struggling to breathe through the ice reached the world via television, one of the strangest and most intense rescue efforts ever seen was launched to save them.

whalers, biologists, oilmen, and environmental-ists you could see concern, enthusiasm, and a true desire to get these whales to safe water. The whalers were especially energized and impatient; they were not going to wait for the hoverbarge. Using long-bladed chain saws donated by an Oregon lumberman, they cut two experimental rectangular holes seaward, where the east wind was now beginning to open the lead. But, as feared, the whales refused to take advantage of the new holes. Arnold agitated the bobbing whale Crossbeak with a pole. "Go over there," he said. Crossbeak swam promptly over to the new hole, but quickly returned to the security of the holes it had helped make.

That night, brilliant, ghostly green curtains of the aurora borealis whipped about the sky, flash-ing in bands tinged with yellow, blue, and red. The wind, from the east at fifteen knots, blew a continuous drift of snow into the air holes, where it quickly turned into slush, then hardened into ice. The seaward hole was completely frozen over. The near-shore hole had shrunk to about ten feet across and was closing fast. It was clogged with ice chunks that rattled like broken glass each time the whales pushed their way through to the life-giving air. Like glass, the chunks lacerated their skin. Bone's breath was shrill and wheezing. Occasionally he rolled side-ways, like a dying goldfish.

A big borough helicopter now beat its way

through the cold air to the site and deposited a bevy of hunters and biologists, along with Minnesotans Rick Skluzacek and Greg Ferrian. Borough phone lines had been deluged by well-meaning callers offering worthless suggestions—such as melting the ice with napalm. After calling and being dismissed as kooks, the Minnesotans purchased their own plane tickets and brought up several of the water-circulating, de-icing devices they had invented.

Accompanied by the biologists, the Minnesotans hauled their little machines to the first hole. Laboring under the light of snowmachines and a portable lamp plugged in to a small generator, the Minnesotans soon had a circulator working. Suspended from a floating foam platform, its little propeller pulled warmer water up from the depths. Immediately, an area of clear water began to open in front of the bubbling de-icer. It grew rapidly. A second machine was turned on, with the same result. Bonnet surfaced, then glided slowly to a bubbler, and to the rescuers. All fell silent. In awe, they gazed at the whale, which gazed back.

Soon the hole was clear of slush and new ice. The hole did not grow larger, but it did stay clear.

The next morning, ARCO got into the act and introduced the Skycrane ice punch. The huge National Guard Skycrane helicopter would hoist the cylindrical five-ton ice punch, the thicker end

Right: On a deeply chilled night when blowing snow threatened to close the holes and kill the whales, two Minnesotans showed up with some water-circulating devices, or "bubblers," which immediately cleared the freezing slush. Afterwards, a whale approached those gathered as if to say, "thank you."

of which hung down over a round smashing platform with a pointed spike in the middle, then drop it onto the ice to knock out a series of holes, which the whales could then follow to open water.

Flanked by smaller helicopters teeming with newsmen, the Skycrane rotored its way over the ice as the heavy punch dangled beneath it. Suddenly the pilot dropped the helicopter almost straight down, breaking its fall with a rotor-stressing jerk only after the punch smacked the ice and tipped over. The Skycrane repeated the process until finally a splash of water shot upward. In time, it smashed out a rubble-filled hole. In the meantime, impatient hunters had taken chain saws to the ice. As the ice punch pounded out four clogged holes, the hunters cut twenty-four neat, clean, rectangular ones.

Still the whales refused to use them.

Gruesome wounds now abraided the whales' skin. All flesh was gone from about the last ten inches of Bone's snout, leaving only bare bone. Whalers and biologists stretched blue and green tarps over the one original hole still open, hoping to force the whales out into the new larger holes. Catching the wind, the tarps billowed like parachutes. Under a darkening sky, the rescuers stood quietly, holding the tarps, waiting.

A blast of whale spray against plastic ended the quiet. The whales looked somehow content

under the tarps, the way a cat does in a cozy enclosure. They would not abandon the old hole.

As darkness crept in the next day, I returned to the whale holes from a helicopter trip out to the pressure ridges of ice, where Morris had sent experts to see if the ridges might be dynamited away. The answer was "no."

I moved down the lengthening line of unused holes to where Johnny Leavitt and Malik worked. Bonnet suddenly surfaced in a nearby hole. "They're moving," someone shouted. A cheer rose. People began running up and down the holes, trying to guess where the whales would come up next.

Having figured out the purpose of the new holes, Bonnet and Crossbeak eagerly moved into each new opening as quick as it could be cut by the whalers.

Then it dawned on everyone that only two whales were surfacing. Crossbeak and Bonnet. No Bone. We never saw Bone again.

Near the dim end of an overcast day, a huge plane, the largest in the world, touched down on Barrow's Will Rogers–Wiley Post International Airport jet runway. Whipping up a great ground-blizzard, brakes squealing, the National Guard C5-A screeched to a stop in the overrun area.

Inside its cavernous interior, the C5-A carried the screw-shaped steel pontoons and other pieces of the Archimedes Screw Tractor, sent by VECO

Left: At first, the grays refused to use the holes cut for them by the hunters. But eventually, they seemed to figure out the hunters' intent and became so eager that they would begin to surface in new holes even before the hunters finished clearing them.

to put a quick end to the hole-cutting. The parts were unloaded under the tail, which hung overhead like giant whale flukes. "If we don't hurry up and get our act together, the Eskimos are going to beat us to the rescue of the whales," a Guardsman muttered.

Word was, the screw tractor would be assembled in time for a test run the next morning. It actually took an extra day, but the test run was made. The machine cut through flat ice with ease, but left a worthless path filled with chunks and slush.

Back at Prudhoe Bay, workers then began to weld a great steel plow. Supported by two trucks or one Skycrane, the plow was designed to scoop out the ice and slush left in the wake of the screw tractor.

Meanwhile the hunters kept cutting holes seaward. Coming from the opposite direction, two icebreakers flying the hammer and sickle now smashed their way through the polar pack toward the whales. Greenpeace took credit for striking up this new alliance. Ron Morris did not dispute this claim.

Crossbeak and Bonnet followed the holes for two miles, then suddenly stopped, refusing to go any farther. The path crossed directly over a shoal where the water measured only twelve feet deep. Many solutions were attempted to lure them across. All failed.

It had now been more than a week since the rescue had begun. It was a beautiful Sunday—subzero temperatures, sunshiny, perfectly still. Church let out. Happy to be free, families motored out by pickup, ATV, and snowmachine to see the whales. Delighted hands reached out to pat snouts. The sun soon slipped below the southwestern horizon and the chill deepened. Mothers and fathers loaded up children, grandparents, and pet dogs and headed home. Darkness set in.

A long breathing hole, beginning and ending in deep water, was now cut across the shallow shoal. Lights and bubbling de-icers were then used as lures to entice the two whales across the shoal. It didn't work.

The next morning, Malik and Arnold Brower Sr. talked to the rescuers. "Think like a whale," they told them. A whale would not swim over this shoal, but it would swim around it. With Malik leading the way, the hunters cut a new path circumventing the shoal.

Finally the two Soviet icebreakers drew near. I flew out by helicopter to document the Soviet effort. From the deck of the *Admiral Makarov*—440 feet long, 20,000 tons—I watched in admiration as the arctic ice that had seemed so formidable gave way beneath the stern. Pressure ridges crumbled. Cracks opened, rippling outward in long, jagged, spider-web patterns through the ice, as far as my eye could follow.

Right: Malik, renowned for his skills as a harpooner and his knowledge of the sea and its animals, seemed to develop a rapport with the gray whales. As the Soviet icebreakers approach, he says what he hopes is good-bye to the whale known as Crossbeak.

As the next day began, optimism overflowed. Whale hunters laughed, joked, and talked to the two remaining whales. Journalists—now numbering 250—flocked about, crowding each other. Sightseers from town patted the whales as though they were pets.

Eagerly the whales began attempting to surface in holes that were still being chain-sawed open. This forced the pole bearers, who were clearing the holes by pushing the fresh-cut slabs under the ice, to wait until the sawers had moved well ahead of them to assure that the whales would not accidently be cut by a chain saw. Malik spoke to the whales as if they understood, telling them they would soon be free.

"Malik seemed to have a rapport with the whales," biologist Craig George later said. "I can tell you one thing I learned. We had gray whale biologists here, all kinds of people, but Malik was the one to listen to."

By now the icebreakers had torn the pressure ridges apart. Word came that they were going to break open a channel in the smooth ice. The hunters began herding everyone off the ice. Soon only Malik and I lingered at the edge of the final hole. The harpooner waited until Crossbeak rose in front of him, then reached out and patted the whale on the snout. "Don't worry," Malik soothed. "We're getting you out of here."

The icebreaker *Arseniev* advanced toward the whales, opening a channel in the flat ice. Sooner then anticipated, the two whales swam four hundred yards under the ice, then emerged in the new channel. Morris ordered everyone to stay away. "I want to give them some quiet," he explained.

Hours passed. The sun descended low. The crowd on the beach was released and everyone rushed to the channel.

Filled with slush and rubble ice, the new channel was quickly refreezing. A pond had formed within the channel. A whale surfaced, blew, rolled in a graceful arch, then continued a rolling swim that took it back under the water. The other followed. An enthusiastic "Hey, hey, hey," interspersed by calls mimicking the cries of sea mammals, rose over the ice as the Iñupiats let loose with the same cheers used to greet crews coming in with a bowhead.

"They look like whales again," a woman shouted.

But not whales out of trouble, for as they tried to advance, rubble and freezing slush slashed their skin, opening up new cuts. They retreated back into the pool, stopped rolling, and began breathing as they had in the holes.

The NBC helicopter swooped down, whipping up snow, which whirled into the pond and quickly became slush, then ice. The whipping wind and flying snow drove back the people on the edge of the hole. An angry cry—"Stop! Stop!"—competed with the whopping of the helicopter blades, to no effect.

Left: As one of the two remaining gray whales surfaces to breathe, the Soviet icebreaker *Vladimir Arseniev* moves in for what everyone hopes will be its rescue.

I backpedaled fast, then suddenly felt the ice drop beneath my feet. I turned to see the screw tractor churning through the ice. It raced toward the channel and the crowd, shooting a web of cracks before it. Cracks snaked out on two sides of me. We sprinted out of harm's way and watched as the screw tractor plunged into the channel, then churned heroically back and forth—doing the whales no good at all.

The hunters regrouped. They felt they could cut a series of holes from the pond to the open lead in short order, then escort the whales there and release them. Vetoing the idea, Morris called in the *Arseniev* for a second pass. Under a moon on the receding side of full, the icebreaker moved back into the channel. Its high-intensity lights blazing through the dusk, the *Arseniev* moved mystically through the twilight-lit ice toward the still-trapped whales.

The mercury rested at twenty below the next morning and would top at minus seventeen. No one knew the fate of the whales. Ron Morris had issued an order for all to stay off the ice.

Working in my darkroom, I kept my ear tuned to the radio receiver. I was surprised to hear an angry Morris scolding Craig George, ordering him and Geoff Carroll, who were convinced the whales were still stuck in the channel, to stay off the ice. Morris said he would fly out at daybreak—about 10:45 A.M. If he did not see the whales, he would assume they had swum safely to open water, and the rescue would be over. Until he gave the okay, they must stay off the ice.

"Well, it's too late now," Craig radioed back. "Geoff's already left." Upon hearing Morris launch into his orders, Geoff had quickly departed. At the channel, Geoff met Arnold Jr.'s brother, Alfred Brower, and a handful of hunters. Together they rode snowmachines along the channel made by the icebreaker. They saw no whales.

Coming back, Alfred moved out ahead. He spotted a vapor cloud in the solidly refrozen channel and rushed to it. There he found Crossbeak in a tiny opening, barely big enough for the whale to raise itself up as far as its blowhole, struggling to breathe. The tip of Bonnet's snout was pushed into the hole, but this whale's blowhole was underwater. Alfred jumped off his snowmachine, dropped to his hands and knees, and began chopping the ice with his pocketknife.

Geoff and the others joined in. After about five minutes, they had cleared an opening large enough to allow Bonnet to slip up alongside Crossbeak. "He took a desperate breath, kind of a big, sobbing gasp," Geoff recalled later. "Normally the whales would stay up for five or six minutes, and take 1.7 breaths per minute. Now they stayed up for twenty-two minutes straight, breathing rapidly, similar to a human's

Right: After inspecting the final track left by the grays in an icebreaker channel, Malik turns away. No one would ever know what fate awaited the two whales once they left this hole.

breath after running in a hard and fast foot race." Once the immediate threat was over, the hunters left to get chain saws. Geoff radioed in to report what they had found. The response was a scolding from Morris.

"Get off the ice! And get the Eskimos off the ice!" Morris ordered.

"It's kinda out of my hands now," Geoff responded. "They've already gone to get chain saws."

"Get the Eskimos under control! Get everyone off the ice!" Morris shouted.

"I can't stop them," Geoff said.

Morris later explained his orders. It would have been better, he reasoned, for all to have waited for daylight, for his flight and assessment. Morris argued that the whales, having become accustomed to men and their machines, might have made a greater effort to escape to open water if Geoff and the hunters had not been there.

"I didn't want human influence," Morris said. "I didn't want chain saws. I didn't want people going on the ice without giving the whales the chance to escape that they deserved."

Alfred and Geoff, however, were convinced that they had found one whale on the very edge of death, with the other soon to follow.

I arrived just before sunrise to find Malik shoveling slush from what could have become the death hole. Nearby, frozen-over breathing holes

were laced with blood, barnacles, and bits of whale skin. When the whales reappeared in the hole, Malik stopped shoveling. As a seagull hovered just feet overhead, Malik bent over Bonnet and placed his hand on a large abrasion. He held it there, silently, his face radiating a look of concern and compassion that reminded me of a father at the bedside of a sick child. The whale lingered under his touch. Malik smiled, sadly.

By noon the hunters had cut a new series of holes to within half a mile of the lead. "We can be there by mid- to late afternoon," Johnny Leavitt told me. "We can watch them swim into the lead, and wave good-bye."

Just then, without warning, the *Arseniev* began to cut a new channel, perpendicular to the chain-saw holes. This channel would soon cross the workers' intended path, cutting them off before they could reach the lead. Hunters and biologists radioed a frantic request to have someone contact the icebreaker and ask it to stop. They were told no one was available who could contact the Soviets.

By mid-afternoon the holes reached the new channel. The opposite edge of the channel was within several hundreds of yards of the lead. The new channel had already frozen over, but it had not hardened sufficiently to walk on. The hunters requested a helicopter to ferry them to the other side so they could continue chain-sawing holes to the lead. Morris denied the request. Frustrated and puzzled by Morris's action, they were forced to stop. Johnny Leavitt wanted to keep the whales overnight in an extra-large hole the whalers had cut, then escort them the remaining short distance to the lead in the morning. Morris nixed the idea and called the icebreaker back in.

—

Well before sunrise the next morning, Craig, Geoff, and I traveled by snowmachine to the site. A short distance out, the icebreakers hovered dimly. Alfred Brower had been the first to arrive. In the early-morning darkness he had raced his snowmachine first toward one icebreaker, then the other, hoping to find out what had happened to the whales, but he was unable to cross the channels the icebreakers had made. Alfred then drove to the long breathing hole. At one end a light, left on as a guide for the *Arseniev*, still glowed. Alfred got off his machine and searched on foot.

He heard a blow, a little to the northeast. He followed the sound and found the two whales, breathing from one small hole in a refrozen icebreaker channel.

Alfred flashed his headlight at the Soviets, who then swept the area with searchlights. One searchlight fell upon the whales. Alfred retreated to the warm-up shack to call in a report. When he returned, the whales had left the tiny hole.

New channels laced the ice in every direction. "This is just what I was afraid of," Craig muttered. "It would have been so simple, just to take

them right out and release them into the lead. For all we know now, they could have gone down any one of these channels, the wrong way."

The channels were filled with chunks of broken ice that were held in the loose grip of a thin layer of hardening slush. The only way to search was to walk about on that rubble of broken ice. It looked to me like a good way to die.

"Step on just the chunks, and you'll be okay," Malik told me. "Step on that thin stuff, you'll fall through. Just remember—walk like a polar bear."

Malik and the other hunters took off at a good clip, hopping from chunk to chunk as casually as children playing hopscotch. I took my time, stepping cautiously. They paused to study the situation, then turned back and searched in the opposite direction. Then Malik found it. A whale track—a spot where a whale had broken through the thin, new ice. Blood, barnacles, and small bits of whale flesh laced the refreezing surface of the track. Freddy Joe Kaleak dug out pieces of flesh with his pocketknife and examined them.

Craig and Geoff had been wandering elsewhere in the channels and had found older tracks, bloody as well. "This could have all been avoided," Craig lamented, "if we had just been able to escort the whales to the lead."

No one would ever know for certain whether the whales made it into the lead and, if they did, what happened to them then. That last, fresh

Right: Soviet seamen aboard the *Admiral Makarov* wave at a North Slope Borough Search and Rescue helicopter filled with media and government officials.

track appeared headed in the right direction. Some people had wanted to radio-tag the whales to keep track of them. Morris had vetoed this strategy, contending tags would cause the whales needless additional stress. But if the whales got stuck again, radio tags could have led to their being found.

We heard the beating rotors of a helicopter. It landed and Morris stepped out. "Under the powers of the Marine Mammal Protection Act, I order everyone off the ice," he stated. "I don't want the whales hearing any snowmachines and coming back." He marched back, grim-faced, and departed.

We stopped by one of the more recent hunter-cut holes. Arnold Jr.'s brother, Johnny, who had dared me to walk on thin ice my first time whaling, jumped on the new ice in the hole and started to dance, Iñupiat style. I jumped on with him. I felt the ice roll like a waterbed beneath my feet. Craig had plunged his heel all the way through the ice to water, right behind me, so I jumped out. This didn't stop Johnny or Craig. They even got down on their hands and knees and made four-legged "polar-bear walks" the length of the hole. "This is how big, heavy bears cross thin ice without falling through," Johnny said. He did a quick little dance, while Craig, Freddy, and Billy looked on.

We then followed the 208 hunter-cut holes, which crossed four and a half miles of ice,

Right: The following summer, stranded gray whale carcasses were found up and down the coast from Barrow. Malik found two that he believed were the same whales he had helped lead to open water. Wryly and affectionately, he gave one a pat on the snout.

toward shore. A bit later, a twin-engine airplane, with Morris in the passenger seat, flew over the lead. Morris spotted no whales. He declared Bonnet and Crossbeak free. The Great Gray Whale Rescue had ended.

⁓

The following summer, a number of gray whale carcasses lay on the beaches north and south of Barrow. About twenty miles southwest, Malik found two together. He believed these might be Crossbeak and Bonnet. He reported his find, then returned to the site with biologists Craig and Geoff. I came along. One carcass lay on the beach, completely out of the water. The tail of the second lay on the beach, its body extended at an angle outward into the water. The biologists took measurements and studied the condition of the whales. The one lying on the beach measured twenty-six feet in length, seven inches off of the in-water length estimate they had made for Bonnet. Malik knelt at its head. A fond smile crossed his face as he gave the dead whale a pat.

After comparing the skin damage and noting the distance the carcass had been pushed up the beach, the biologists concluded this was not Bonnet, but rather a whale that had likely died the year before the rescue effort. The other dead whale measured more than forty feet, compared to the thirty-foot estimate the biologists had made for Crossbeak.

Not long afterward, Malik recalled the rescue and told me that when I had witnessed him chatting with the whales, he had heard them speak to him. "'Malik, we're scared,' they tell me. 'Malik, we're scared. Help us, Malik. Help us.' I tell them, 'Don't worry. It's going to be all right. We'll get you to the lead. You'll be safe there.'" And in the eyes of this whale hunter and whale rescuer, I saw tears.

Right: As the rescue fades into history, Roy Ahmaogak, whose discovery of the three gray whales had set off the whole spectacle, gives his son, Bennie, a haircut as Tiger the cat walks by.

"Our people
don't really need
much in the way
of training. They
are natural born
hunters. They know
the country real
good. The real
training they get is
when they go out
hunting and fishing,
from the time they
are babies."

—JIMMY NAYAKIK

SHORTLY AFTER Public Works employee Harry Norton drove his D-9 Caterpillar tractor into the surf to try and save Uncle Foot, he packed a sled, hitched it to his snowmachine, and drove inland to hunt caribou. He failed to return on schedule, but this was his way. Eventually, however, too much time passed. His family grew worried. Harry had last been seen October 5, and they notified Barrow Volunteer Search and Rescue on October 15. A search was launched.

Volunteers from Barrow and Atqasuk launched a ground search by snowmachine. Randy Crosby, director of the borough's search and rescue agency, launched his helicopter to look for campsites along the Inaru River.

On the afternoon of October 16, Crosby's spotters located a campsite near the river. Drifting snow had covered a blown-down tent and some red gas jugs. The site was forty-three miles south of Barrow, seventeen miles north of Atqasuk. The team landed and found a hunting shirt, sleeping bag, and duffel bag with personal gear in it—all belonging to Harry.

The search then fell under the jurisdiction of the Atqasuk Volunteer Search and Rescue and its director, Whyborn Nungasuk.

From his earliest days, Whyborn had followed his father into the country to hunt caribou and onto the ocean to hunt walrus, seals, and whales. He observed the behavior of animals and watched his father's hunting technique. When Whyborn was seven years old, his father decided it was time Whyborn learned to do things himself. He took Whyborn out into the country and dropped him off, alone, with a tent and a rifle, for one full week. "He just leave me a little food," Whyborn recalled. "When that run out, I still got to eat, so I got to kill caribou. Nobody's going to teach me how, I just got to do it. Sometimes I cry; I'm getting hungry. I start looking for even small game. Squirrel. Small birds. I sure am hungry." He got his game, and with it a priceless and increasingly rare education.

Whyborn and his dog, Chubby, were helicoptered out to establish a field station near Harry's campsite. He brought his sleeping bag, some frozen fish, caribou, whale, his knowledge of the country, the dog, and nothing else. Later he would get a radio and Coleman stove, but he could not wait for these. He had a lost man—a husband and father—to find.

In the air, Crosby, his partner Price Brower, and the other search-and-rescue pilots found themselves diverted by other missions. Two hunters were overdue from a trip along the Chip River. A fall whaling crew was stranded by a storm. An asthma victim was struck down in a remote camp; a ten-year-old Nuiqsut girl had suffered head injuries; a trucker was injured in a rollover along the pipeline highway. All required rescue.

Yet the pilots persisted and finally found Harry's sled along the river, thirty miles from Barrow. Further searching on the ground turned up his snowmachine, which had fallen through the ice of a creek.

On October 20, Whyborn's ground crew found Harry's footprints on a lake about two miles north of the sled. The following day, Crosby was flying eight miles from where the snowmachine had been found when a tiny object

jutting out of the snow caught his eye. It was Harry's thermos bottle.

Later that night, a body was reported lying on the sea ice offshore from Barrow. Crosby helicoptered out and directed a strong searchlight down upon it. The body's head popped up. The body rose to its feet and headed toward the beach. It turned out to be a non-Native who had come from far away to go to the ice, there to commune with God. Shortly afterward, the wind pushed this ice back out to sea. Had Crosby not found the man, he would indeed have greeted his maker.

⌒

About this time, I returned to Barrow from a visit home to Wasilla, Alaska, where I had heard nothing of the search, which was now twelve days old. Mayor George Ahmaogak suggested I cover the search for the borough magazine. Price Brower, a short, stout, boisterous fellow with a quick sense of humor, gave me a lift to the site in a ski-equipped Cessna, loaded with food and supplies for the searchers.

As we flew through a white universe, Price pointed out where the snowmachine and thermos had been found, then noted the field rescue camp in the distance. It was more than eighteen miles from where the submerged snowmachine had been found and the most recent place Harry's footprints had been uncovered.

Price cranked a wheel protruding from the floor. The plane jerked suddenly as the skis

Previous page: After Harry Norton's snowmachine was found under the ice of a creek, volunteers from several villages undertook the slow, deliberate process of following the trail he left, uncovering his tracks one at a time.

Right: During the search, North Slope Borough Search and Rescue aircraft were diverted several times to assist in other emergencies. Flying as a spotter on another mission, Raymond Neakok keeps his eyes peeled for a lost father and son, who were ultimately rescued in good health.

■ **Left:** Harry Norton poses on the Cat he had so bravely driven into the surf in the effort to save Uncle Foot.

dropped into position beneath the large tires. We descended from five hundred feet to thirty feet above the whitened tundra. Price shot over the top of the tents, lifted up, looped back in, dropped down, and felt for the invisible runway beneath his skis. The Cessna bounced high, took a short series of hops, then stopped. I climbed out and jumped right onto a sled that would take me out to the searchers.

It was one of those white-out tundra days that make you feel like you are inside a giant eggshell. A sky, musky-white with obscured clouds, folded into the tundra, which was buried in wind-whipped snow of the same shade. No visible horizon separated sky from earth. No shadows fell to give shape or texture to the drifted plain. On such a day, a trail of white-on-white-wrapped-in-white can disappear even while you walk on it. Perspective dissolves into deception. Distant objects appear close, and nearby objects, far.

The activity unfolding before me seemed extremely odd and desperately futile. Stretched out across the tundra in a thin, staggered line, a group of men wielding household brooms were sweeping snow.

This was snow that had fallen in a dustlike, seemingly dry form that had been whipped horizontally over the tundra until the tiny granules encountered obstacles with enough resistance to wrest them from the wind. Where these obstacles were no more than short blades of grass, the snow accumulated to depths no greater than a few inches. But where the wind met stubby mounds of frost-heaved earth, riverbanks, or a hunter's cabin, the snow piled into drifts ranging from one foot to more than fifteen feet high: hard-packed drifts so sturdy that you can walk over one and not sink, leaving behind only the faintest of footprints. Sometimes a boot will break through the hard surface and plunge into the drift. When the wind is blowing, which it usually is, that same boot can be pulled out as you watch the new track fill with drifting snow and disappear. This happens even when not one fresh snowflake has fallen for weeks.

"You better get some snowshoes on, if you're going to walk around out here," volunteer searcher George Kingik told me. I retrieved one of several pairs of aluminum snowshoes sitting on a sled and lashed them to my boots with a band of rubber cut from an inner tube. I then followed George to a point a short distance ahead of the last banner of a zigzagging trail of flags staked into the tundra. In the opposite direction, the trail of flags disappeared into the whiteness.

Angling the outside edges of his snowshoes downward, George began to dance up and down on the hardened snow, cutting into it and breaking it up. Once he had broken up a sufficiently large area, he used a broom to sweep away the broken snow. This done, he crouched. Eyes

intent, he studied the surface he had just uncovered. He found what he was looking for and signaled another searcher, who brought a flag and planted it at the spot.

"Take a look at this," George said. I squatted beside him.

In the flat light at first I could see nothing, but after careful scrutiny I made out the faint imprint of a boot heel and then a boot toe.

"That's Harry's footprint. Push on it," George said. But I did not want to destroy something so priceless, found at such great effort. "Go on, touch it with your fingers. Push on it," George urged. Reluctantly I did so, putting three fingers right through what appeared to be the ball of the foot. "Push on the heel." I did, timidly and gently. This was a footprint that had been made two or three weeks earlier. Two blizzards and many windy days had since covered it under the drift, seemingly erasing it and its maker forever from the sight of other men. Yet George had found it. "Push hard!" he scolded. I pushed hard. The boot heel did not yield.

"You leave a print out here and it gets as hard as cement. You can't sweep it away," George explained. "We know these things about our land. Our grandparents were born on this land for thousands of years, and we know it. I haven't been to work for twelve days, but I can't stop until we find Harry. None of us can."

Bit by bit, these men were restoring Harry's trail, which was now nearly twenty miles long. George was tired. They were all tired. No one had any thought of quitting.

"Bill!" I was suddenly jarred by a loud shout behind me. I jerked around to look into a full, lightly freckled, smiling face atop a short, muscular body. "Did I startle you?" Arnold Brower Jr. laughed.

I guess he did, a bit.

Previous page: Having already spent twelve days uncovering twenty miles of Harry Norton's footprints, searchers continue looking.

Left: A flag is placed over a newly uncovered footprint.

Right: After breaking up the drifted snow with their snowshoes, searchers sweep it away to uncover another track left by Harry.

"It's funny to hear English," Arnold said after we exchanged pleasantries. "I haven't spoken English for days. There's some extra brooms on that sled over there."

I replaced my cameras with a broom and joined the searchers, who moved slowly but steadily across the tundra, freeing Harry's footprints from the snow.

Gradually the searchers approached a low, frozen marsh. A small group broke away and ventured ahead into the marsh. They soon signaled that they had found more tracks. We kept right on working where we were. "We have to be sure," one man told me, "that those are his tracks. And not someone else's."

Another half-hour passed until the men in the marsh signaled that they had positively identified the tracks as Harry's. All the rescuers moved in that direction.

With archaeological precision, the searchers were excavating what appeared to be a campsite—no fire, no tent, just a place where Harry had slept. Below the snow was solid ice in which tracks stood out distinctly. It had been slush when they were made. Less than a hundred yards away, a shallow embankment rose out of the marsh. Snow blowing over it had piled to a depth of several feet.

A small group of searchers moved up to the drifted embankment. They prodded it with long poles. I joined them. James Toovak prodded the

snow with an iron rod, then stopped. "Here he is," James said. He waved and shouted at the others. "He's right here." Standing atop a rise behind him, another searcher lifted a hand and signaled to other searchers unable to see James.

All came running over. With hand, broom, and shovel they cast aside the drifted snow. Soon a patch of brown corduroy material appeared, then the fur ruff of a parka. The search for Harry Norton was over. I felt my heart pumping extra blood into my head, leaving me a little dizzy. All present bowed their heads as the elder, Mark Ahsoak, began to pray over the body. His words were Iñupiaq, their literal meaning unknown to me, but the feeling and spirit were clear. The cold air was saturated by a feeling of sorrow, and relief, and the awe one feels when faced with the knowledge that a person has left this realm for whatever lies ahead. I was amazed that they had found Harry at all amid this stark, featureless landscape. I doubt any other group of people in the world could have done so. Love poured out of the elder's prayer—love for the man and his family, love for the land and environment that gave the people life and that so easily took it back.

Digging out the body was a quiet, sacred work. When it was done, the searchers stood in a ring around the deep hole, leaning on their shovels and, with solemn eyes, paying their respects to a fellow hunter who had died doing what they all

Left: "Here he is!" the shout goes out after the body of Harry Norton is located under a deep drift.

do. I looked from the body up to the face of George Kingik. His head was bowed, but his open eyes radiated sorrow and humility.

"Thank the Lord!" a voice cried, finally breaking the quiet. "Praise God!" another echoed. Hands reached out and joined in warm clasps. The toughest men I have ever known threw their arms around each other in deep embrace and wept.

After a bit, Johnny Aiken walked up to me. "I've never seen a dead man before," he said solemnly. I knew he had been to a good many funerals, but I also knew what he meant.

Glenn Roy Edwards, who had been scouring the countryside on a snowmachine, arrived. I followed him and Johnny down to Harry's final campsite in the marsh. Near a small upthrust of tundra, slightly less than two feet in height, Glenn Roy helped sweep the snow off a set of impressions that at first meant nothing to me. Glenn Roy studied them, then placed his boot toes into two of the impressions. They fit nicely. He dropped down and let his knees fill two other imprints. He was kneeling directly in front of the upthrust. "It looks like he might have tried to build a fire right here," Glenn Roy speculated, though there was no sign of matches or of fire.

Finally he leaned forward and placed his forearms in two impressions atop the upthrust. "It looks like he was praying," Johnny said.

Later, Arnold Brower Jr. came over. He inspected Harry's prints, and likewise positioned

■ **Right:** "Thank God," someone sighs. "Praise the Lord," another echoes. Then all gather around the remains of their fellow hunter as the elder, Mark Ahsoak, offers a prayer.

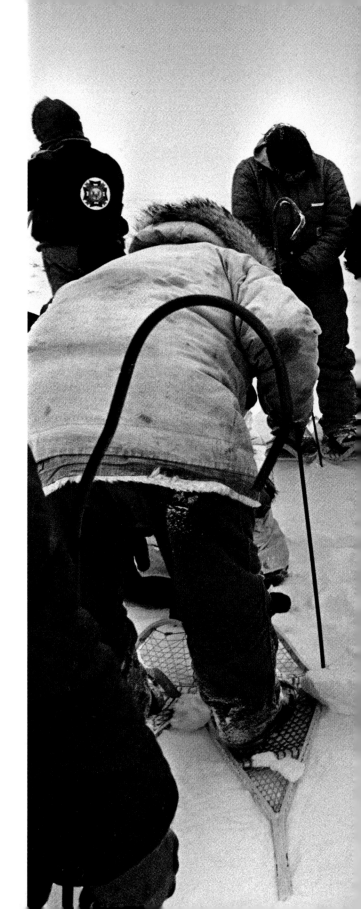

himself in them. "This is where he prayed," Arnold confirmed.

The snowmachines and sleds had been moved to a point a bit above the death scene. People stood about talking quietly, sitting on snow-machines, leaning against sled backs, or resting on sleds. I let my weight slip down against the back of a sled. George came over and sat down beside me. He looked tired, worn. It was time for him to go back to his home village of Point Hope, time to go back to the office.

"What did you think of this search and rescue?" he asked. I told him how impressed and moved I felt.

"This is our land, we know it, and we love it," he said, repeating his earlier sentiments. His voice trembled, his eyes watered. "When this happens, we have to stick with it, the different villages. Until we find them. We know our people, we know this land that we love so much. We know this land."

A bit later, I sat down next to the elder. He spoke of past searches and of what the rescuers had gone through. He recalled a search many years before. An old man had dreamed that a lost man had drowned and now lay under the ice. They tracked him and found him, drowned under the ice. "It's real interesting," the elder said. "It's a good work to do."

The roar of a snowmachine carrying a woman sitting behind a volunteer rose over our conversa-

tion. Together the searcher and the woman dismounted and walked up to Harry's body. The woman began to weep. She fell to her knees and mourned. The elder ran over and put his arms around her.

About 4:00 P.M., as a dim day slipped into the extended arctic twilight, a helicopter brought a police officer. The little group gathered together. The elder spoke a while, in Iñupiaq. Heads were bowed, hats removed. Low sobs emanated from some searchers. The elder prayed again.

The police officer, a middle-aged white man, appeared nervous, self-conscious, about the task he had to perform in front of these people.

"It's all right," one said. "Go ahead. Do your job." And so the body of Harry Norton was photographed and placed into a forensic body bag, which was then zipped into a larger, bright-orange bag and loaded into the helicopter for his final trip home.

That night I set the alarm for 7:30 A.M., went to bed, and laid awake until an hour or two before that time. When I finally tumbled into a troubled sleep, cast in white, a broom appeared before me, sweeping snow into snow, into more snow.

Left: After becoming lost in a May blizzard, a group of women and children out hunting geese were found, some on the edge of hypothermia. Tears of relief fell as thankful relatives embraced them at the Barrow airport. Many owe their lives to the efforts of volunteers and the North Slope Borough Search and Rescue team.

"I dream belugas
swim by and then a
whale. A beautiful
whale, pushing big
water up by its
side. The next time
we go out of the
tent, that whale
come to us."

—Kunuk

BY 1986, as a result of the hard scientific and lobbying efforts spearheaded by Iñupiat whalers, Barrow's annual quota for bowhead whales had risen to seven strikes. The first six strikes were made in rapid succession, with three of the whales landed.

The seventh strike was made by Jonathan Aiken Sr.—Kunuk—and resulted in the landing of a thirty-six-footer. I first heard of the catch while I sat taking notes at a Tuesday evening meeting of the North Slope Borough Assembly. Sally Brower, who handled contracts made under the mayor's office, suddenly excused herself and motioned for me to follow.

She soon tore across the ice on her snow-

machine, towing a sled onto which I clung. We traveled southwest, parallel to the beach, on flat ice for about fifteen miles. Then we turned seaward, continuing through a series of pressure ridges until we came to a broad plain of flat, young ice and turned back to the northeast. Long before we reached them, we could see a line of people straining to hoist a whale from the water, although no water was visible; they were pulling the whale up through a hole in the ice. The pullers tugged at a thick rope attached to a block and tackle. The whale was mostly up.

As we came into camp and stopped, someone from another crew was pulling out, towing an umiak. Plenty of whales were running in the sea. Barrow hungered for more than the four landed whales the seven strikes had yielded. Yet the quota had been filled. The hunt was over. This umiak would be of no more value this season.

I jumped off the sled and went running for the whale. Just as I reached it, it was pulled completely out of the water, onto the ice. The people dropped the rope, and as one, moved toward the whale.

Clad in a white, fur-lined parka, Kunuk walked through a joyous crowd of people reaching out

with congratulatory handshakes and hugs. He stopped in front of the bowhead, which lay stretched out upon the ice. In front of him, Bowing his head, he offered a prayer of thanks. Then this middle-aged grandfather leaped onto the tail of the whale and climbed atop its midsection. Kneeling there, he stretched out his arms. Someone in the crowd handed him a toddler. Kunuk cuddled young Jordan Aiken securely at his right side and, with his left arm, scooped up another, slightly older boy, Derren Aiken.

Together, the three of them—hunter and grandsons—looked out over the crowd, which responded with cheers, applause, and the taking of snapshots.

The open lead of water was separated from the landing site by a broad plain of young ice, strong enough to support men but the not the weight of a bowhead. After taking the whale, the hunters had cut a series of small holes from the lead to this site of older, stronger ice. A hook connected to a long pole was dipped into each successive hole and was used to snag a heavy rope attached to the whale. In this manner, the bowhead was towed under the young ice to the edge of the more sturdy ice.

Here a large hole had been cut and a simple but strong handmade block and tackle had been attached to the flukes of the whale. Community members then joined together in pulling on the thick ropes. "*Kiita!* All hands! Walk away!" The

Previous page: With April comes the spring, and with the spring, the open lead, and in the lead, bowheads. Standing behind his umiak, Kunuk waits for the whale he hopes is coming to him.

Left: As the women see them off, Kunuk tows the umiak and leads his crew down to the ice and the beginning of their journey to the lead.

cry had gone out again and again until at last they pulled the bowhead up through the hole and onto the ice.

Sitting atop the whale with his grandchildren, his blue flag with the yellow smiley face flying from an ice perch behind him, Kunuk struck me as a hunter of skill and as a compassionate man. I knew I wanted to document the activities of his crew for *Uiñiq* magazine.

I made my request in writing but received no definitive answer. Spring gave way to summer, summer to winter, and finally it was spring once again. Kunuk, his family, and his crew were loading up their sleds and their skin boat—the umiak—with the camping supplies, tools, and weapons needed for the hunt.

Feeling depressed that whaling was about to begin and that I was without a crew to follow, I stopped by Kunuk's house. I would see them off and say good-bye. Maybe next year it would work out. Maybe staying in town in a warm house, with a warm bed to sleep in, wouldn't be so bad. I could still get out to the ice and take photos every time a whale was caught. It wouldn't be so bad. Maybe when the next season rolled around, a crew would take me in.

Kunuk had already given out candy to all the children who had come to see his crew off. A long rope connected the umiak to his snowmachine. Heavily loaded sleds were attached to the other snowmachines. Clad in parkas covered

with the fresh white of newly sewn hunting shirts, the hunters had already climbed onto their machines and were ready to pull the tug ropes.

Kunuk looked at me. His eyes, hidden behind sunglasses, gave me no clue as to his thoughts.

"You coming?" he asked.

⌒

My first year following Kunuk proved uneventful. The quota for Barrow stood at seven strikes. Six went fast—at other locations. Soon only one was left. Kunuk and his crew waited at the water's edge in tense eagerness, poised to launch the umiak at a moment's notice, hoping to be the crew that would bring that last whale home to Barrow. Their hopes were dashed by excited voices crackling over the radio, telling us the final strike had been made twenty miles to the north by the crew of George Ahmaogak. We listened for about an hour as hunters in boats chased the whale. "Hey! Hey! Hey!" the happy cheer finally came, then a prayer. George Ahmaogak had his whale.

From the seven strikes, four whales had been landed. Whales continued to pass by, but the hunt was over. Two hunters left to help with the butchering. I stood alongside the umiak with a sad and resigned Johnny Aiken, Kunuk's oldest son. The umiak had never hit the water. I could feel his discouragement. A bowhead surfaced in front of us. Johnny watched silently as it headed off toward Canada.

Right: The Wainwright crew of Ben Ahmaogak Sr. stalks a whale that surfaced a short distance down lead from their camp.

Previous page: Ben studies two bowheads.

Left: In the village of Kaktovik, all whale hunting is done in the fall (from late August to early October), when the sea is open. As the mountains of the Brooks Range loom in the background, a tiny aluminum skiff carries a crew to a bowhead.

"We go home now," he finally spoke, softly. We packed up camp and left.

Elsewhere on the lead, the crew of Burton Rexford found itself in an awkward position.

"We were just informed through CB that some crew had just struck the last of our quota for Barrow," Fred Kanayurak, one of Rexford's crew members, later related. "Minutes later, maybe three or four, a whale surfaced within a few yards in front of our boat. One of our crew, Takak, through instinct and experience, had grabbed one of the weapons and was upon the whale with an intent to strike. Someone tried to convince him that there were no more strikes, but still he tried to pursue. We thought he was going to strike. I could hear someone saying, 'No! No! No!' I couldn't withhold my tears from falling down my cheeks, feeling the strong commitment of our crew member for the purpose of sharing. I'm sure there were others that were watching, with tears in their eyes. I never felt such a weakness surging through my body. Finally he yelled—still upon the whale— 'Doesn't anybody have ten thousand dollars!?'"

Takak knew that a lawyer for AEWC had speculated that a person who struck a whale beyond the quota might escape jail time by paying a fine of ten thousand dollars.

Aivik, another captain, had struck and lost a whale. He refused to give up. For five days he prowled the waters wrapping around Point Barrow, going from the Chukchi Sea into the Beaufort. Finally he found his whale, dead. It had drifted more than fifty miles from where he had first struck it. Insulated by its thick blubber, the decaying insides of the whale had heated up, filling with gas and steam. It was now a stinker. The meat and internal organs had spoiled. Still, the maktak—the black skin and the attached layer of blubber—would be good. It had been chilled by the cold water and protected from the internal heat by the thick blubber. Upon hearing the news, other boats came out to help. It took a full day to tow the large whale back, and more than another day to haul it up onto the ice and butcher it, but now there was more maktak to pass throughout the community.

Back at the Aiken home, I helped the crew divide their share of the Ahmaogak whale. Each crew member received for his family about enough

Left: Standing in the front of the boat captained by Herman Aishanna of Kaktovik, Freddy Kaleak readies the harpoon as they approach a bowhead.

Right: Ben Ahmaogak strikes an already-harpooned whale with the bomb-firing darting gun, introduced by Yankee whalers in the nineteenth century.

meat and maktak to last one week, maybe two with rationing. They would be given more of this whale at the spring whale feast of Nalukataq and at Christmas and Thanksgiving, but it would not be enough.

A week later, the hunters of St. Lawrence Island ended their hunt. Weather conditions had prevented them from making their last strike, so the allocation was passed to Barrow. Soon we were back out. The lead was wide, ducks abundant, the whales fewer in number and mostly far out.

The majority of the bowheads pass by the coast in three separate pulses, beginning with juvenile whales of twenty years or fewer, ranging from about twenty-seven to thirty-eight feet, and ending with large whales that can be a century and a half old, sixty feet long, and up to eighty tons. This was the time between the second and third pulse. No whales had been seen for a while.

We soon learned that this final strike had been taken by a camp far from ours. Again Johnny Aiken stood at the ice edge, looking over the sea. Again we saw the breath of whales, more distant this time.

Left: A little misjudgment places the boat of a Wainwright crew in a dangerous spot. Harpooner Dave Ahlalook chooses not to use the darting gun.

Right: After finding success, Ben Ahmaogak (left) is congratulated by his brother and fellow whaling captain, Fred.

And again Johnny's voice poured out the soft, sad lament, "We go home now."

The *Aaluut* gave up on the hunt for that year and moved inland to hunt geese.

———

Two crews did stay on the ice after this whale was taken: those captained by Simeon Patkotak Sr. and Percy Nusunginya.

Simeon was convinced God would provide him a whale, a legal whale, regardless of the quota. In a later year, I would see Simeon's faith in action when the east winds opened the lead early. Whalers moved out and did some hunting, but then the wind shifted to the west and closed the lead. It stayed closed for a week, then two. As the third week drew to a close, whalers grew

Left: Whalers prepare to tow the whale caught by Ben Ahmaogak's crew back to the ice.

Right: Hunters from the Colville River village of Nuiqsut venture seventy miles to establish their fall whaling camp on Cross Island, just offshore from Prudhoe Bay. Having successfully taken the last of their allotted three strikes, they tow the bowhead taken by the crew of Thomas Napageak back to the island.

worried. They gathered on the beach to pray. Standing at the forefront was Simeon. He prayed mightily, beseeching God to turn the winds back to the east, to let them blow upon the ice and open up the lead once more.

After the prayers, I called the National Weather Service. "Any hope for an east wind?" I asked. "No," came the answer. "We see these conditions persisting for as far into the future as we can look ahead."

Two hours later, I passed by the airport and to my great surprise, the windsock had made a 180-degree turn. The wind blew from the east, very gently. It quickly gathered strength, rising to twenty-five knots. It blew and blew, until finally the lead opened. Simeon and the others went out to get their whales.

This spring, however, Simeon had heard a small, quiet voice whisper in his ear, "Simeon, this year you're going to get a whale."

"How, with the quota filled?" he asked.

"A strike will be passed onto Barrow from another village," the voice told him. On a Sunday in mid-June, Point Hope gave up its last strike, which was then passed to Barrow. The lead was wide, and Simeon could see whales sounding in the distance. He faced another dilemma. In honor of his God, Simeon does not hunt on Sundays. Wondering what to do, he consulted his Bible. He found a certain scripture. Yes, he concluded, the sabbath ends at 9:00 P.M., which

was drawing near. At 9:00 P.M. sharp, Simeon launched his aluminum boat and motored out to meet the whale he was certain was coming to him. At 10:00 P.M. he met that whale. He struck it, killed it, and accepted its gift.

The year's quota was again completed, and the official hunt was over. But Percy Nusunginya was determined to let no rules created by politicians and bureaucrats in distant places interfere in his relationship with the whale. If a bowhead was coming to give itself to him, he was going to be there to meet it and to accept its gift. And, in a later year, this is exactly what happened. Percy took a whale after the quota had been filled and the hunt had ended.

As a result, the Barrow Whaling Captains found themselves in a hard position. Not a single one thought the quota that Percy had broken was just. Not a single one believed that the authority of the outside world to dictate numbers to them had the moral authority of their aboriginal right to hunt the whale. Yet recognizing the power of the government, they had entered into an agreement with the National Oceanic and Atmospheric Administration. This federal agency had agreed to allow them to manage the hunt, providing they honored the quota and enforced it upon their own people. Percy had never recognized that agreement as valid.

Reluctantly, his fellow captains turned Percy over to federal authorities for prosecution.

■ **Previous page:** Ben Ahmaogak's daughter, Mary Ellen Bodfish, dances for joy as boats towing a whale caught by the Wainwright crew of John Hopson return to the ice.

■ **Right:** After landing a whale, Simeon Patkotak raises his hands in a joyous greeting to those waiting on the ice.

Being a man with a strong sense of honor, Percy did not fight the charges. He admitted what he had done, and he was then expelled from the Alaska Eskimo Whaling Commission. He pleaded guilty before U.S. District Court Judge Andrew Kleinfeld in Fairbanks. He interpreted the proceedings to mean he would later be allowed to argue the constitutionality of his case at higher levels, and that the U.S. attorney's office would recommend a punishment that would include no fine and no jail time.

When Percy returned for his sentencing, he found himself facing quite a different situation. Kleinfeld sentenced Percy to two months in a Fairbanks halfway house and fined him three thousand dollars. Kleinfeld placed Percy on probation for three years, ordering him not only to abstain from whaling, but to stay off the ice altogether.

Shortly before he was to serve his jail time, I stopped at his house. "My father hunted whales, my grandfather hunted whales; I want my son to hunt whales," Percy told me. "We were never

Left: In a different time, John Hopson sat in the open door of a helicopter in Vietnam, gripping a machine gun, firing and being fired upon. Now, he sits alongside his daughter, Iluktune, surveying the whale that he has brought back to her and to his village.

Right: John Hopson Jr. helps secure a block-and-tackle pulley system to a whale taken by the crew of Andrew Ekak, as Steve Patkotak pushes loose ice away with his fiberglass kayak.

taught to run away from a whale when it comes to us. I am whaling to feed my family and my community."

On May 5, Percy's son John walked under the bowhead baleen arches held up to honor all Barrow High School graduates. His dad was not there to witness this big moment—he was serving his time in Fairbanks. Shortly afterward, John joined the Navy and was sent to the Persian Gulf to help wrest the oil reserves of Kuwait from Saddam Hussein.

When John returned, his father turned his boat and crew over to him, making John the youngest whaling captain in Barrow. John took his role seriously. Up to that time, it had been the practice to set up trash pits behind whale camps, out of sight of approaching bowheads. When the season ended, many crews would strike camp and pull back, leaving the waste dumps to drift off with the ice and disappear into the vastness of the Arctic. At one time all the waste was organic and was consumed harmlessly back into the environment. Now it included pop cans and plastic. John saw the practice as a violation against his beloved Arctic. He introduced a resolution before the International Whaling Commission, requiring all trash to be hauled back into town. He argued passionately for its passage.

The older whaling captains listened. The resolution passed unanimously.

While John agreed to abide by the cooperative agreement and the commission's jurisdiction, his heart remained with his father. "Whaling is very strong in our family. It's been in our family for thousands of years," he told me. "My grandfather, my great-grandfather—they did not abide by numbers. Why should I abide by numbers set by people thousands of miles away? My grandfathers hunted in harmony with the whale. We hunted in harmony, without outside interference."

John recalled how his father had blacked out the first time he caught a whale, though not in such a way as to fall down unconscious. The people around him did not even know he had blacked out. By all appearance, Percy was functioning as normal. Yet he had no physical awareness of himself or his actions. He did not come to until he found himself on the ice, butchering the whale. Percy concluded he had died with the whale and then come back with it. "My dad went through this each time a whale came to him," John said. "I'm waiting for my first whale, waiting to see if I will die with it, as my father did, and then come back again."

Dark clouds hung low over the ice as I followed Johnny Aiken, who in turn followed his father, Kunuk. It was my second year with the crew. We swung picks and chopped our way through the pressure ridges toward a narrow, even darker band of clouds. We had set up a temporary

Previous page: The flag of Burton Rexford's crew is planted atop a pressure ridge as a beacon to all who are driving their snowmachines down from Barrow to help with the hauling out and butchering.

Right: Whalers prepare to haul out a whale taken by Barrow's Tukle crew.

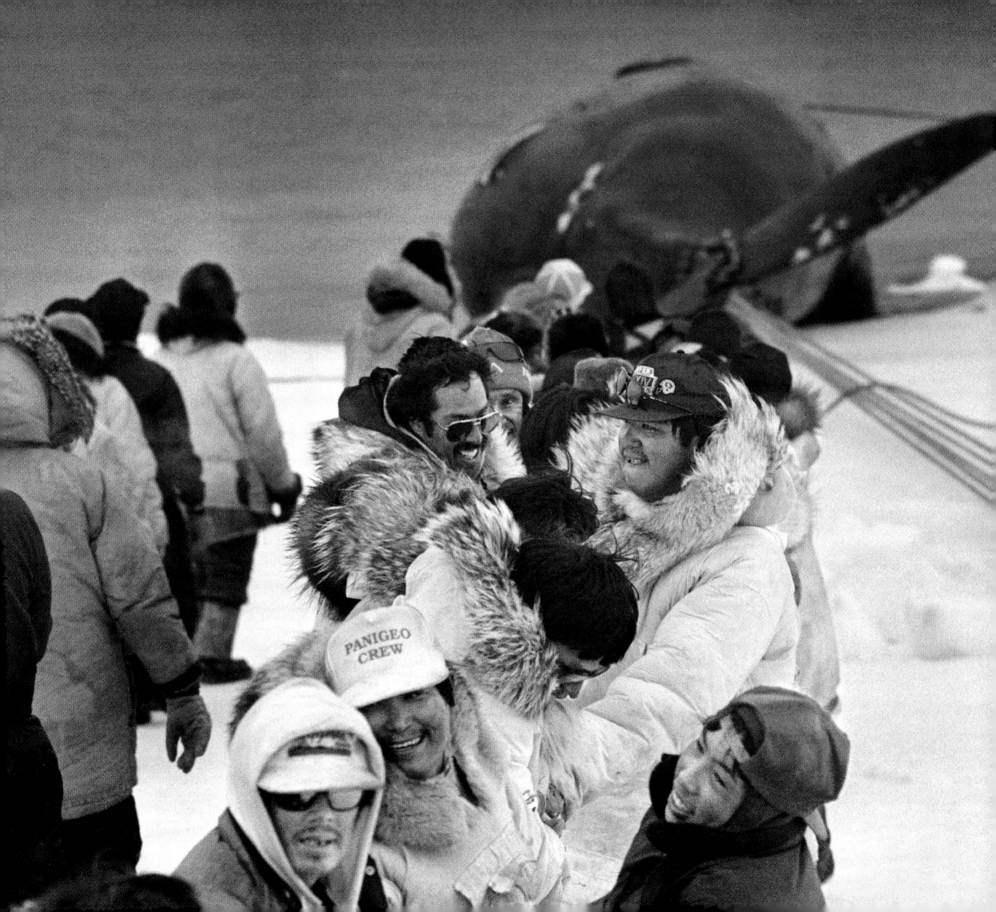

camp on safe ice the night before. There had been no open water, but the wind blew briskly from the east. To the north of us a lake had opened in the ice. Two or three bowheads had been spotted in it. No one would hunt them, for if they were struck but not instantly killed, they would almost certainly move out of the lake, under the ice, and be lost.

A bank of very low clouds often hangs over the ice. Where there is open water beneath, with no ice and snow to reflect light back up, the

clouds appear dark and heavy—"watersky." Now, the dark bands of watersky ahead told us the lead was beginning to open.

We chopped our way to where the thick shore-fast ice gave way to a broad expanse of thin, broken, slush ice. We stopped. This appeared to me to be a barrier we could not pass. The ice had frozen to a thickness of less than one inch, then had been struck by the forces of wind, current, and advancing ice. It had crumpled and broken into tiny pieces that were

Left: Although it is hard work—it can take whalers as many as twelve hours to haul a whale out of the water—it is a happy task, generating many smiles. Few angry words are heard when a whale is being hauled out.

Right: After anchoring a block and tackle in the ice, "all hands walk away" again and again until the whale is hauled out onto the ice.

now being welded back together by the freezing slush. Joined by fellow whaling captain Jacob Adams, Kunuk studied this ice, then to my amazement began to nimbly and confidently pick his way across by placing his feet only on those clumped-up piles of rubble that his educated eyes told him would hold his weight. Jacob followed Kunuk. Johnny followed Jacob.

I had no desire to follow, but I did not want to miss anything. So I followed Johnny, taking care to place my feet only where his had been. I was convinced that with one misstep, a man could slip beneath this rubble and never be seen again.

Finally we could see the lead, less than a hundred yards ahead of us. It was no more than ten to twenty yards across in the widest place, and widening so slowly that the movement could not be seen. We saw no whales. The whalers studied the conditions for some time, then turned back toward more firm and stable ice.

Most of the other crews were still back in Barrow. It was April 25. No whales had been

Left: As midnight nears, Kunuk poses with his grandsons, Derren and Jordan Aiken, atop a whale that has come to him.

Right: Following a long period when the west wind has kept the lead closed and prevented any whale hunting, Simeon Patkotak prays for an east wind. "No chance," said the weatherman. Yet, hours later, the wind shifted, blew hard, and opened the lead.

caught this early for a number of years.

We set up a new camp on safe ice, about one mile north. A short distance from the tent, running along the line where the more solid ice joined the rubble, was a series of ice peaks reaching up about twelve feet. I sat down outside the tent to relax and read comic books. I noticed Kunuk, Jonathan Jr. (Johnny's younger brother), and Claybo Solomon standing atop these peaks, scanning the distant open water for whales. I put Sgt. Rock aside and joined them.

"We saw two whales already," Claybo told me. I watched for fifteen minutes, seeing nothing. Kunuk climbed down, pulled the starter rope on his burgundy-red Ski-Doo, and drove off to the north, scouting for a good site to relocate camp come morning. In front of us, the dangerous rubble extended seaward for about four hundred yards, to where the lead slowly grew wider as the wind pushed the pack ice farther out to sea. I was surprised to spot Eli Solomon working his way through this rubble, beyond the distance we had gone earlier, all the way to the very edge of the water.

Suddenly a small black triangle drew my eyes into the narrow lead. A V-shaped spray rose into the air above it, then drifted slowly back down to the ocean. The graceful curve of the whale's back rolled beneath. "Bowhead!" I shouted in a whisper, although it was not really necessary to be quiet at this point. Claybo and Jonathan Jr.

smiled, and laughed good-naturedly at my reaction. Soon another bowhead came, and another, and another after that. But with this dangerous rubble in front of us, it was impossible to reach them.

Jonathan Jr. returned to the warmth of the tent. Claybo and I stood alone. The wind tore at us from behind, ruffling the edges of our parkas. Occasionally, in the distance, out beyond the tumbled rubble ice, another black line would break the surface, shoot off a blast of vapor, and then be followed by the great rounded hump of the back as the whale dove.

Between whale sightings, Claybo spoke of his days in the military, his travels Outside, to Asia and Germany. He had enjoyed it. Especially Germany. The people there had been good to him. He had enjoyed experiencing the warm weather and taking part in many kinds of entertainment. He had seen a variety of country: mountains, forest, crowded cities, sunny beaches.

Then a whale appeared. Claybo stopped talking. Another followed immediately behind. Together the two bowheads lingered for about fifteen minutes.

"This is the best place in the world," Claybo said. "That's how I feel about it."

Kunuk then returned. He had found a new campsite.

Kunuk went into the tent, pulled out tools, parts, and explosives, and began making the

Right: Brothers Raymond and John Hopson Jr. help begin the butchering of a Wainwright whale landed by Andrew Ekak.

bombs that are shot inside a whale to hasten its death. Next to him in a large Ziploc plastic bag was a neatly folded flag, colored a deep navy blue. A yellow smiley face and the name Aiken were emblazoned across it.

Randy Edwards, Kunuk's fourteen-year-old grandson, watched closely. Occasionally Randy would ask a question about bomb-making. Kunuk would respond in his quiet, calm voice. There were two apprentice hunters in camp this year: Randy and Ned Nelson—the same Ned Nelson who, the year before, his first ever out on the ice, had fallen off a sled I was towing. I did not notice his absence for about half a mile. When I returned to pick him up, I found him hiking nervously across the ice, imagining himself as dinner for a polar bear.

Outside, Johnny, Claybo, and Jonathan Jr. carefully removed the kinks from the long rope attached to the brass shaft of the harpoon, then

Left: A fluke from Ben Ahmaogak's whale.

Right: Baleen from a whale that came to Arnold Brower Jr., who, honoring Iñupiat tradition, gave the credit to his elderly father and captain, who had been unable to be on the ice at the time.

wrapped the rope around a large, pink, globe-shaped float. They started at the bottom, then continued up in neat, even coils that eventually covered half the float. The coils were secured in place with string that would easily break, allowing the rope to uncoil should a bowhead drag it into the ocean.

When I awoke the next morning, Kunuk was already out on another scouting mission. He returned and announced he had found an even better location. Quickly the hunters dismantled camp, packed sleds, and roped the sleds to snowmachines. No one was grouchy; everyone was in a good mood. This is just how I had

Left: Two whales, one taken by the Arnold Brower crew and the other by that of Simeon Patkotak during a fall hunt, are butchered on a Barrow beach. By September, the perpetual light of summer has yielded to a day and night of average length.

Right: Having spent more than forty straight hours hunting, towing, and hauling out a whale, Wainwright captain Rossman Peetook catches a short nap before going at it again.

always heard it should be in order to convince a bowhead that this was a fine crew, one that would honor it and be worthy of its gift. Excitement, anticipation, and goodwill radiated from everybody.

Kunuk always ran a respectful camp. With him I could imagine it being no other way. Before

coming to the camp, his ice cellar had been thoroughly cleaned. I witnessed no fighting or bickering in Kunuk's camp. Kunuk seldom issued orders. Hardly ever did he tell anyone what to do. He would begin working, and then everybody, knowing what was expected of them, would do the same.

Left: When whaling quotas have kept the take of bowheads artificially low, Barrow, home to the world's largest Eskimo community, has often found itself short. Members of the Aiken crew pose with the shares they will take home to their individual families, from a whale caught by George Ahmaogak.

Right: Even as the whale is butchered, its *maktak*, boiled to become *uunaalik*, gives whalers such as Moses Nayakik of Wainwright the energy to stay warm.

Clad in his white hunting parka, William Sielak braced one Sorrel boot against the wooden sled, took hold of the rope that weaved back and forth over the load of camping gear atop the sled, and with a mighty tug tied it down. He stood, turning his face into the east wind. "I feel really good today," William said. "A whale is coming. I can feel it. Someone is going to catch a whale today." He didn't say "we"; that would be like boasting. Tradition teaches that whales do not like it when people boast about how they are going to catch them. But there was

Left: The Aiken crew watches intently as another crew down lead paddles after a bowhead. The whale slips by them.

Right: As the same whale reaches their camp, the Aiken crew members prepare to launch.

a light in his eyes, a smile on his face.

Hunters driving snowmachines fired them up, and those riding sleds climbed on. Kunuk took the lead, towing the umiak. Looking sharp in their white hunting parkas, the hunters fell in behind.

The ice was rough and broken. The crew had to stop frequently to cut trail. Eventually we neared the campsite Kunuk had found. I had expected this to be a place free of the rubble we had camped by the night before. I was wrong.

Although frozen somewhat more solidly, it was rubble of the worst kind. I could see no way to travel on it.

Between us and the lead stretched a chaotic-looking jumble of small pressure ridges made of rubble ice, shielded on all sides by thin slices jutting out in every direction like a tangle of ragged, frosty razor blades. Wind or current coming just a little too strong from the east could easily break this field of rubble apart and carry it into the

Left: The Aiken crew pursuing the whale.

Right: After the whale passes them by, the Aiken crew cleans the slush off their paddles before it grows hard and becomes ice.

lead. Coming from the west, the same forces could crush it into piles. The Aiken crew parked their snowmachines, took up their picks, and began chopping their way through several hundred yards of this rubble toward the lead.

This wasn't like going through the big pressure ridges, cutting passes through high mounds of ice. It was all low, jagged ice that looked like it would cut you in half if you fell on it. Every foot of the way had to be cut, each shard of

Previous page: The Aiken crew searches for another whale.

Left: A whale comes to Kunuk, and he thrusts the harpoon. Eli Solomon follows with a shot from the shoulder gun.

Right: Smoke fills the air, and the kick from the shoulder gun knocks Eli backwards.

thin, broken ice—welded together by frozen slush—had to be cut down, one at a time.

It was about 11:00 A.M. when we reached the campsite. I was soaked in sweat. I was hot now, but I knew that in my wet clothes I would shortly be freezing. I remembered the year before when I had gotten so cold on my thirty-hour watch. I had grown so miserable that at times I was convinced I simply could take no more. I had said nothing, uttered not one word of complaint, had taken it and had survived. This year I knew I would take it and survive too.

The work of setting up camp had just begun when a pod of belugas swam by. We stopped to watch. Minutes later a bowhead broke the water just to the north of us. The boat was not ready yet, so the hunters could do nothing but watch. Soon the tent was staked. Caribou skins covered the floor. Claybo tumbled onto them and fell asleep.

Kunuk placed an experimental, factory-made, high-shock bomb designed in Norway into the darting gun, which protrudes from the end of the harpoon shaft alongside the harpoon itself. As the harpoon penetrates whale flesh, the darting gun is triggered by contact with the whale and fires the bomb deep into its vital areas. Eli armed the other weapon—a big, brass shoulder gun—by sliding one of the black-powder bombs Kunuk had made the night before into the broken-open barrel. He snapped it shut. It would be Eli's job to follow the harpoon strike with a second shot from this hand-held cannon.

Kunuk then laid the darting gun in place at the front of the umiak, the harpoon extended beyond the bow. The rope attaching the float to the harpoon was wrapped in a neat, flat coil on a platform just inside the bow. Hand-carved paddles were wedged into place between the ugruk skins and the cords binding them to the umiak frame.

Before the umiak could be positioned, a whale came. Waving his arms frantically, Johnny signaled crew members still hauling gear through the rubble to turn off their snowmachines. Kunuk and the available hunters hurriedly grabbed the gunwales of the umiak, pushed it to the edge of the ice, and shoved off. Randy stayed behind and, overcome with excitement, lost his breakfast between two chunks of upturned ice.

The bowhead dove and was not seen again.

Claybo ran out of the tent, irritated that he had slept through the first chase. "I am not going to sleep again," he vowed. "No way! Not until we catch a whale!" I remembered previous seasons passing with no whale at all. Claybo could become one sleepy hunter.

As we finished setting up camp, another whale blew. A second chase ensued. The whale vanished.

With camp finally set up, it was time to change into dry clothes. I carefully removed my parka. In one pocket I placed a camera with a telephoto lens; in the other pocket I put a camera with a wide-angle lens. I placed the parka just

Right: After a whale is harpooned in Kaktovik, Fenton Rexford fires the shoulder gun to hasten its death.

■ **Left:** The final breath of a bowhead. Its rain of blood brings life—for both the body and spirit—to the Iñupiat people.

inside the tent, by the flap, hoping to keep the cameras warm enough to guarantee they would shoot, but far enough from the tent's warmth and humidity to protect them from fogging up.

I sat down on the grub box and pulled dry clothing from my duffel bag. I removed my boots, socks, and warm outer garments. Soon I was stripped down to just an undershirt and lightweight inner pants. Suddenly the tent flap whipped open, revealing Johnny's flashing eyes.

"Whale!" he whispered excitedly. I jammed my feet back into the boots and yanked my cameras from the parka. In this state of near undress, with my untied boot strings flapping free, I slipped outside.

Quickly I shuffled to a position behind and to the left of the boat, which was still on the ice. I was startled to see, just yards in front of the umiak, the triangular hump of a bowhead, gliding silently toward the umiak. Crouched low in the bow, grasping the harpoon, Kunuk waited for it. Just behind Kunuk, Eli sat, gripping the shoulder gun. The rest of the crew crouched on the ice around the umiak, ready to shove it into the water.

I had long been told a bowhead gives itself to a good-spirited crew—that this animal is so smart, grand, and powerful that even the best crew could not kill one unless it first gave itself to them.

In spirit, I had always accepted this concept. In intellect, I had reasoned that it was solely the hunter and crew with the most skill and stealth, those best able to work together, who would get the whale.

What I now saw inflated my spirit and rose beyond my intellect. The whale appeared to bow in front of the umiak. It looked and felt to me as though it were offering itself to Kunuk.

As quickly and silently as possible, I scooted behind the boat to the backside of the windbreak. As I did, I heard the hollow, scraping sound of wood and hide grinding against ice, then the splash of the umiak as it entered the water, followed by the blast of the last breath of the bowhead.

I popped my head over the windbreak. Kunuk had raised his harpoon. Eli had lifted the shoulder gun into firing position. Kunuk thrust the harpoon into the whale, a bit behind the head. As the harpoon sank in, the trigger to the darting gun made contact with the bowhead's skin, firing the bomb deep into the whale's body and blowing the heavy, wooden harpoon shaft arching back over Kunuk's ducked head. Eli followed close behind with a shot from the shoulder gun, sending another bomb into the whale. An explosion flashed out the barrel. The kick knocked Eli off the seat and onto the floor of the umiak.

The whale disappeared. Tense seconds crept by. Nobody moved. The shock of the two bombs exploding reverberated through flesh, water, and ice. Johnny and another crew member,

Jonas Solomon, ran back across the ice with the float, unraveling the rope as they went. William Sielak sprinted close behind. More tense seconds passed. Then the whale rose to the surface, rolled onto its side and, raising a flipper into the air, told us its spirit was about to shed this parka. It had given itself to Kunuk's crew.

Left: As Kunuk sees the whale has given its gift to him, he raises his hands in a shout of joy and praise.

Right: Claybo Solomon and Johnny Aiken clasp each other in a joyous embrace.

Kunuk lifted his hands above his head and shouted in joy.

"Thank God!" someone shouted. Suddenly everyone was clasping hands, hugging, laughing, crying.

Tears burned my cheeks, making it hard to focus. Perhaps a few of these tears were for the death of this great animal; yet in that death I had witnessed something ancient and beautiful—I had witnessed a gift of life, of culture, and of spirituality, given by a whale to men.

I had witnessed the gift of the whale.

■ **Right:** "Then the whale rose to the surface, rolled onto its side, and, raising a flipper into the air, told us its spirit was about to shed this parka."

■ **Following page:** After the hunt is over and they reach flat ice near the shore, the young men of the Aiken crew race home.

EPILOGUE

EPILOGUE

Left: Belugas pass by a hunter's blind offshore from Point Hope.

MY INTRODUCTION to the Iñupiaq whaling culture culminated in Kunuk accepting his gift of the whale, but it did not end there. I spent two more seasons with Kunuk's crew, then ventured off to see how other villages hunted bowhead. In Point Hope, I was taken in by the crew of Elijah Rock and his son Rex, known as Kakianaaq. The spring I traveled with them, Elijah and Kakianaaq landed a whale.

A month later, I joined them and the other Point Hope crews for *Qaqrugvik*, their three-day whale feast. As I observed the food preparation, prayer, blanket toss, and traditional dancing—and especially the pride on the faces of the captains and their families as they freely distributed the bounty the whale had given them to all who had come, and the happiness on the faces of those who received it—I realized I was in the midst of something extraordinary and beautiful.

The thought struck me that perhaps somewhere deep in the forgotten histories of all people, we might have shared in something similar; in a belief that wealth and status is defined more by what you give to others than by what you hoard for yourself. Somewhere along the way, most of us lost this belief. To fill the void, we created churches, clubs, fraternities, and organizations of many kinds, but we never managed to come all the way back to that earlier history. Far from ideal, modern life in Point Hope is beset by many social problems. Yet here in the catching of the bowhead whale and in the ancient traditions that go into the distribution and sharing of it, I did find something ideal.

In Kaktovik, Herman Aishanna let me ride along in his skiff, the Green Boat, as he helped the crew of James Lampe Sr. kill and land a bowhead during a fall hunt. The next fall I was scheduled to follow the whalers of Nuiqsut, who stage their hunt from tiny Cross Island, just off-shore from the oil fields of Prudhoe Bay. The day before my planned departure from my home in Wasilla, I took the Running Dog up for a test flight. All was in good order. I touched down so smoothly and perfectly that I was suddenly over-come with an urge to bring the plane to a record short stop, so I slammed full force on the brakes.

I did come to a record short stop—one that left the Dog protruding tail up on the runway, nose into the ground, propeller bent. Nuiqsut had an allocation of three strikes that year. As I searched for another propeller and had it mounted, the hunters landed their first whale. I then winged my way north, but bad weather forced me to overnight just south of the Brooks Range. As I waited for good weather, Nuiqsut landed its second whale. Two days later, as I

Left: After receiving his whale, Ben Ahmaogak returns home, exhausted. As he sits in his favorite chair, his daughter's beagle, Sadie, crawls onto his lap.

Right: During Barrow's spring whale feast of *Nalukataq*, members of the Aiken crew join hands with those of three other successful crews as a blessing is offered over the flesh of four bowheads.

pulled within visual range of Cross Island, I heard shouts of celebration and joy from the Nuiqsut whalers crackle over the radio. The third whale had just relinquished its gift to them.

I spent another spring season following the crew of George Ahmaogak of Barrow, and then for the next season I traveled, unannounced, to the village of Wainwright. There I met a whaling captain, ready to go out on the hunt. In his polite and friendly way, he made it clear he did not want his crew burdened by the presence of a photographer.

I walked on. I came to the house that Benjamin Ahmaogak Sr. had built. He had

Left: Jimmy Frankson, Point Hope artist, with one of his carved walrus tusks.

Right: The late Eileen MacLean of Barrow is presented with a fish while campaigning on the Kobuk River. The state house district that she was elected to serve covers a piece of the Iñupiat homeland the size of California, encompassing the North Slope Borough, as well as lands south of the Brooks Range where trees grow.

already passed out his candy and was ready to go whaling. This kind, highly energized, silver-haired man took me in. One of the truly great whalers of all time, he and his family treated me as though I were blood kin. Their home became my home. In sharing their successful hunt with me, they gave me what would become one of the outstanding experiences of my life.

Although never as frequently as I desired, I got to follow many other hunts—for caribou, seals, walrus, geese. I went on fishing trips and, following hunters plucking murre eggs from precarious ledges, scaled cliffs rising nine hundred feet straight out of the Chukchi Sea.

These for me were magnificent times, unlike anything I had ever experienced in the world of

■ **Previous page:** At the beginning of the twentieth century, villages often celebrated good hunting seasons by inviting other villages to come and share in *Kivgiq*, a "Messenger Feast" celebrated with dancing and gift giving. The tradition disappeared until the 1980s, when it was revived in Barrow. Here, Wainwright dancers perform *Kalukaq* during the feast.

■ **Left:** Paul Tazruk of Point Lay, who once saw a ten-legged polar bear, drums at *Kivgiq*.

■ **Right:** Robin Mongoyak of Barrow, drumming for *Kalukaq*.

sport hunting and fishing or of recreational hiking, backpacking, and canoeing, however grand these activities sometimes prove to be. I was with modern people, bound by an ancient tie to the land and sea.

I also saw the darker side of life here: the alcohol, the drugs, the long, long, long nights in which sleep is continually disrupted by the cries of someone lost in the perplexities and confusions of the modern world. For example, a young person once showed up at my door in the dark of forty below, begging for help that I could not give—that no one could give—as we so painfully learned not long afterward when he lifted a gun and ended his own life.

Yet for periods of time, I saw these kinds of social problems virtually disappear. I saw pride and pleasure overpower the frustration and anger in people's eyes. I saw people smile, laugh. I saw even the most bitter of political rivals put aside animosity in honor of the bowhead, join hands on a common rope, and with their community pull as one to haul in the whale's bountiful gift, which they in turn gave out for no dollar paid in exchange.

I saw this joy and goodwill continue into the feasts and celebrations, conducted without the artificial stimulants of alcohol and drugs but instead with the real stimulant of knowing you are participating in something ancient and good, something of value to yourself and your community.

At the same time, I heard outside voices, voices without understanding, cry out against this great tradition. I heard the argument that no human should kill a whale, or any animal, although the continued life of those making the argument depended on the continued death of animals, whether they realized it or not. I heard those who believe in hunting but who follow the odd creed that the mere fact that they are Americans, are Alaska citizens, gives them a right to the traditional resources of Alaska's Native peoples equal to that of the Natives themselves.

I have heard it said the Iñupiat can get their food from the store. Store-bought foods have their place, but they do not satisfy; they do not warm and energize the body as does the oil of maktak.

And what about the values behind the hunt? Can these be bought in a store?

There are other threats to both the bowheads and the Iñupiat way of life, such as the noise and potential spills of offshore oil and gas development, and the apparent climatic and ecological changes of global warming manifesting themselves in Arctic seas by warming water and thinning ice pack.

Then there is the force of the all-permeating modern popular culture itself. Will children drawn to the same TV shows, computer games, music, fashions, and junk food as other American children be able to find the inner will required to face the hardships of whaling?

Previous page: The future of the whaling tradition will soon rest largely in the hands of a new generation. Barrow boys unleash their energy playing along the rotted beach ice of June.

Right: The state champion Tikiaq girls of Point Hope.

I look at some kids and wonder; then I see
young people breaking trail, cutting freshwater
ice, cleaning camp, catching their first seal or
goose and giving it to an elder. I gain new confi-
dence in them. Adults have always looked askance
at the young, yet the young manage to grow up
and carry on.

Ultimately, time and circumstance compelled
me to move on and leave the bowhead hunt
behind. Yet these whales continue to swim
through my dreams. I wake up, pained by a
deep longing for a way of life that belongs
to someone else.

Left: Susie Akootchook of Kaktovik dances with her sister, Jane Thompson.

Right: Bowhead whale.

Left: Late at night, during the whale feast of Nalukataq, Forest "Big Boy" Neakuk is tossed off skins taken from a successful umiak. Earlier in the day, the girls visible on crutches had been hauled away by ambulance following bad landings during the children's blanket toss.

Right: Jana Harcharek gives her son Nagruk a blanket toss preview.